ROSES FOR A STRANGER

Reread June 2007 Pauline. + 2010 re-read a blessing each time.

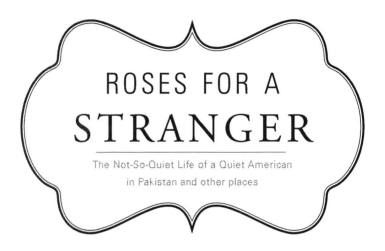

ROSES FOR A
STRANGER

The Not-So-Quiet Life of a Quiet American
in Pakistan and other places

KENNETH G. OLD

TATE PUBLISHING & *Enterprises*

Roses for a *Stranger*

The not-so-quiet life of a quiet American
in Pakistan and other places

> *I've no desire to go*
> *Where springs not fail,*
> *To fields where flies*
> *No sharp and sided hail*
> *And a few lilies blow.*
>
> *Instead my feet shall go*
> *Where stings the hail*
> *And to those lands*
> *Where droughts prevail*
> *And stunted children grow.*
>
> *And, maybe, a few roses.*

Kenneth G. Old

TATE PUBLISHING
& Enterprises

Tate Publishing is committed to excellence in the publishing industry. Our staff of highly trained professionals, including editors, graphic designers, and marketing personnel, work together to produce the very finest books available. The company reflects the philosophy established by the founders, based on Psalms 68:11,

"THE LORD GAVE THE WORD AND GREAT WAS THE COMPANY OF THOSE WHO PUBLISHED IT."

If you would like further information, please contact us:
1.888.361.9473 | www.tatepublishing.com
TATE PUBLISHING & Enterprises, LLC | 127 E. Trade Center Terrace
Mustang, Oklahoma 73064 USA

Roses for a Stranger

Unless otherwise noted, scripture quotations are taken from the Holy Bible, King James Version, Cambridge, 1769.

Scripture quotations marked "NEB" are from The New English Bible, The Delegates Of The Oxford University Press And The Syndics Of The Cambridge University Press, 1961, 1970.

Poetry excerpts are from Footprints in the Dust by Kenneth G. Old.

Cover design by Lindsay Behrens
Interior design by Chris Webb

Published in the United States of America

ISBN: 1-5988697-1-X
06.12.04

Enough

Enough –
To have walked each moment
As touching the Ineffable,
Dragging its hem,
Spotless and white
And maybe reluctant
Into the frenzy and filth
Of our tangled hours.

The stories told in this book are as true as fallible memory permits. Where possible and appropriate they have been checked with individuals involved in them. Names of people and places have sometimes been changed. Immaterial details of the stories themselves have also sometimes been altered.

Royalties received by the author from the sale of this book are dedicated to the education of poor children who live in the Land of the Five Rivers in Pakistan

Dedicated to

the Strangers among us,
like Marie and Mac,
Brend and Marjet,
Cyril and Margaret,
Kalim, LeRoy, Phil,
Stuart and Homer
who show us that
it is indeed possible
to touch
That which is Beyond
and bring it back
to where we others are

UZBEKISTAN   TAJIKISTAN

TURKMENISTAN   CHINA

                                    Gilgit

                          Peshawar   Skardu
        Kabul ◉   Taxila
AFGHANISTAN   Islamabad ◉   KASHMIR
                      Bannu   Rawalpindi
                              Jhelum   Jammu
                        Gujranwala ●
                              Sialkot
                  Zhob   Lahore ●
            Chaman   Zafarwal
                          Falsalabad

        Sibi   Bahawalpur
    Nok Kundi
        Dalbandin   New Delhi ◉

IRAN   PAKISTAN   Khairpur   INDIA

            Bela
                Hyderabad ● Mirpur
                Karachi   Khas

ARABIAN SEA

Table of Contents

Foreword

By Dr. Robert D. Leggett, admirer and friend of Ken, Marie and Patty

You are about to embark on an adventure of a lifetime, guided by that master storyteller, Ken Old. If you have read any of his previous books, you are already experiencing a "rush" of anticipation of another soul-searching and God-filled journey. Ken feels that God brings people to their remote door in the English countryside, no matter who they are, with and for a purpose—His purpose. While they are visiting he is out to help them discover what that is and sometimes even he is surprised at what is going on in the heavenly mind.

Roses For A Stranger is a book about a saint—Marie Johnson McGuill Old.

No, I didn't find her on the Internet list of those sainted by the Catholic Church, but anyone who has spent even five minutes with her and anyone reading this book will readily agree—she was a saint. Even though she is not among the listed, her life sings with qualities of saintliness.

Her story is exquisitely portrayed by her second husband. He himself may well be considered her partner for sainthood but that is a story for some other time and place.

The lives of Marie and her two husbands, Mac and Ken, have been skillfully woven into the Pakistani setting of most of the book. They worked out their lives among people far different culturally from themselves, but were knitted together by the one God over all and the uniting and stimulating fellowship of the Sialkot Mission that they served.

More about the lives of Christians in Pakistan can be found in Ken's earlier books *Walking the Way*, *A Boy and His Lunch* and *So Great a Cloud*.

Ken has an unusual relationship with God that enables him to hear God talking with him about his life and, more importantly, about following God's directions! Although an engineer by training, he is led through his relationship with Marie into becoming a missionary and Marie's partner in a fascinating modern missionary tale.

Roses for a Stranger is filled with examples of God's providence bringing to pass His purposes. It leads to reflection on whether similar instances are, or could be, happening in our own lives.

Among Ken's other talents are gifts of imagination and poetry. For example, take his complete ease in fusing together fantasy and reality. I have seen Ken mesmerize adults, as well as children, by his tales of the *Little People*. These seven heroic creatures are only half-a-thumb high but even so guardians of truth and righteousness. Hopefully, these fantasy stories will also one day be published.

The full collection of his poetry, *Footprints in the Dust*, is a valuable devotional tool in its focus on the changing relationships that occur between men and God. *Roses for a Stranger* gives an opportunity to savor some of this poetry.

During Marie's stint in the Mediterranean theater during World War II, she served on hospital trains in Africa and Italy. In addition to her excellent nursing skills, she brought to her task the strength and encouragement of a strong Christian faith wherever she went. One could listen for hours as she related her war experiences.

In 1947, the setting for Marie's life changes forever. God leads her to volunteer for a medical missionary group going to India/Pakistan—an area rife with turmoil over the partition of India but one made to order for saintly actions. In the new country of Pakistan her romances with Mac and later Ken flourish.

Ken draws upon Mac's detailed journals to show how God takes control of a young man's life and brings him to India. Mac has already served six years as an unmarried and happily adjusted missionary associated with the Sialkot Mission. After he marries Marie in 1948, they work together in a Mission Hospital in the northwest of Pakistan.

Continuing the influence of Marie's life beyond her death is this book itself. All royalties from the sales of this and previous books are going into a fund to educate the Punjabi children that Marie once labored to help.

Marie Old

Introduction

The title of this book is taken from a long poem in the collection *Footprints in the Dust*. The poem, written over a period of time in the early seventies, discusses the nature of Godliness exemplified to us by certain gifted *Strangers* among us. Often during a long Urdu sermon in the chapel, I would divert my attention from the preacher to scribble a verse.

Rather than any one particular individual, the *Stranger* mentioned in this poem is a composite of several people who have intrigued me not so much by their capacities as by the spiritual quality of their lives.

They live like *Strangers* from the rest of us. They know and experience things in a different way. They see differently. They experience God in a way that I envy for myself.

They exemplify the spiritual life lived out among the shouts and screams of busy bazars, the soiled rupee notes of eastern commerce and the oil, grease and smoke of the various shunting engines of our modern day.

The spiritual life is man's primal Call and his purpose for being. It is the reality we hear calling dimly in our sleep, which we try to capture in ill-remembered dreams. We try to rally to its trumpet call ere we wake and find that yet once more we have lost it.

Every care, every concern, every worry and the weight of each responsibility that breaks upon our freshly wakened mind weaves inexorably a blanket. It is a blanket that, instead of warming, damps to ashes the fire we strive to keep alight each morning with hope to hold its flame throughout our day.

Yet, and this is our surprise, the spiritual life is not a life of unreality but instead, a life of reality enhanced by a splendor beyond ourselves. It is a life oriented towards God that never takes leave of those roots that lie within our own mortality. It does not find sustenance in asceticism or in withdrawal from or in negation of the joys and pleasures He gives to every man. It is not a life of dreams that separates the dreamer from the doer, but rather a life of dreams captured and placed within the vital template of our active waking day.

Unless we live a life of the spirit, our whole individual human enterprise becomes a chasing after shadows and a pursuit of rainbows. It is not the spiritual life that is illusory but rather the life lived without it. The insubstantial and eternally insignificant persuades us it alone is solid and too often we believe it.

There is however, out beyond us, ever beckoning us, an order of reality transcending that of normal experience as a hilltop is higher than the lake below. This reality is not protected by a door to which we have no key. The life of the spirit is the key, the door and the journeying way itself.

This integrates us into the real order established by God. We know of its truth and intimate and absolute reality by the *Strangers* who move around among us. They discover and display to us reality as it really is, not as we imagine it to be.

Because of what they are, they reveal to us also what we ourselves could be. They make us aware of our possible own real selves and place those new and shining selves in the very presence of a fresh discovered God.

They have a charisma that is not transiently bright. Instead it cuts through and illuminates their mundane surroundings with a revealed and sustained glory. Somehow, when you encounter them, you feel you have been privileged to meet God through them.

On our outer side
We touch the world
And on the inner
God.
Some are so closely
Side by side
Light shines through
From one side
To the other.

They are ordinary men and women who, in some indefinable way, have become extraordinary. They are not as rare as we might think and you yourself probably know some of them. Take time to pause and name them to yourself.

These Strangers, who cross our paths
All too infrequently
Have been enabled
By the splendour and might of Him
Working within themselves
To know the One who calls them
To the mysterious way.
Reality has broken through
And they reflect His likeness.

The ones I know are not necessarily great achievers; I don't know that you would call any of them great. Not all of them are Christians. However they each had something extra, a sense of *Presence* with them, and it is that something extra the poem struggled to describe and which this book itself might clarify.

It is after Marie dies that I realized the story of this remarkable woman's life is in my mind and in my heart and in mine alone. If I do nothing, then something of more than personal significance might slip irrecoverably away. This book is, then, amongst other things, a bouquet for my own particular and very precious *Stranger*, Marie.

Prologue

In simple terms, this book is largely, although not entirely, a series of glimpses into the lives of several foreigners who lived in Pakistan and made that land their own during the latter part of the twentieth century.

It is both an adventure story and a romance, primarily about three people. Although not one of them was a Presbyterian, eventually each of them became a missionary of the tiny Sialkot Mission of the United Presbyterian Church of North America. They spent their working lives in association with it in the Punjab province of Indo-Pakistan.

They turned their lives over to God in vastly different circumstances and from childhood places thousands of miles apart—the crowded suburbs of New York and the mountains of Montana in the United States and across the ocean to the beaches of Cornwall's north coast in England. They worked out their lives in one of Asia's newest nations born of dreams and bloodshed during the partition of India in 1947.

A peculiar conversation took place between me and, what might you say?–an angel?—during the night of December 11th, 1949. I recall only a few words of it. The rest of my life was to be governed by its consequences.

I was a civil engineering student close to completing my course. I lived in lodgings near the center of Plymouth in England, sharing a large front bedroom with a bus driver. I did not consider myself a Christian.

It was probably about 2:30 am. I was suddenly awake, alertly awake. I listened intently. What had wakened me?

I could hear Keith the bus driver breathing heavily in sleep in the other bed. I could see the moonlight coming through the window but my portion of the room was in shadow. Someone, someone unseen, was standing at the right hand side of my bed, two or three feet away. I could see nothing of or about the visitor. I just knew he was there.

A voice spoke, a man's voice, a normal voice, no dialect to notice but positive and firm in tone. Loud enough to hear easily. It was a statement, not a question.

> *"Ken, God has a purpose for your life.*
> *"He is going to put you to work in a land that is not your own land, amongst people of a different color and race and culture and creed and He is going to put you to work amongst boys and He is going to bring it to pass."*

My mind raced. I believed in God so it was in His Hands to have a purpose for my life *BUT* . . .

I recall nothing other of the conversation except my own reply.

"Give me three years first and God can have the rest of my life."

I said it, I meant it and I never swerved from it.

On the same day that I had a night visitor in Addison Road four strangers to me were making their preparations for Christmas. They shared the same house in a Mission hospital in Taxila in the north of Pakistan, a new country that was a product of the breakup of India. The village in which they lived, a hundred miles to the east of the Khyber Pass into Afghanistan, had a history of several millennia. Its Hindu king, Ambhi, had once made a pact with Alexander the Macedonian as he marched through from Ohind on the Indus to the rivers Hydaspes and, ultimately, the Sutlej. The village had been a center of Buddhist culture and learning in the days of Asoka, the pre-Christ emperor.

Mac and Marie McGuill had returned to Taxila only three months previously after their marriage in the States. They were planning their Christmas trip to Kohat in north Waziristan where later they were to be located to carry on evangelistic missionary work. Mac had dreamed of this move ever since his arrival in India eight years previously. It was one step closer to his ultimate goal of Afghanistan.

Norval and Dorothy Christy had, with a second summer in Landour in India, completed one year of language study and still were hard at work studying whenever duties in the hospital eased. Norval was a pediatrician but was being constantly stretched by the variety of surgical needs impressing themselves upon him. Because of the snows recently fallen in the hills to the north, patient numbers were diminishing, giving opportunity for Christmas shopping expeditions to Rawalpindi twenty-two miles away.

This story tells of them, most particularly of Mac and Marie. It is also my own story of a twenty-year journey towards a divinely orchestrated appointment and what happened at journey's end.

Marie Johnson

Marie Johnson is the daughter of immigrants who come from Sweden toward the end of the nineteenth century. She is born in Butte, Montana, U.S.A. just one week prior to the outbreak of the First World War.

The girl's developing years are split between Ronan, Montana and Selah, Washington.

When Marie is just nine, her secure and happy world on the homestead in Montana with her parents and her brother, the only world she has known, is turned upside down.

Clara, her mother, has required a hysterectomy. Although the operation itself appears successful, Clara has become mentally disturbed. The isolation at the homestead has not helped. Sam and the two children have done their best to manage the home and the farm and at the same time care for Clara. The home they can manage but Clara's irrational behavior continues to develop. When the children are both at school, Sam has to be always within Clara's immediate vicinity lest she harm herself or lose herself.

Charlie, Sam's older brother, and his wife, Ida, come out from Selah. There is a family conference. Things cannot continue as they are going. It is decided that Clara needs to be committed to an institution that will manage her care, that it will be too much for the little girl to be without her mother and that Marie shall return to Selah with her uncle and aunt and go to school there. Sam and Bill will remain and manage as best they can.

Selah lies on the Yakima River which rises in the Cascades and flows south and east into the Columbia. There is there a community of fruit growing immigrants with Swedish background, including Uncle Charlie and his family, where she is welcomed. Aunt Ida will fill the role of mother for her that cannot be filled in Ronan. From the age of nine through middle school, her years are spent on the fruit farm in Selah. Her father is able to come from Montana and see her only rarely because the livestock on the homestead need constant attention.

Her first cousin, Lillian, twenty years older than she, becomes her close friend and a role model. They share a room for a while.

It is from her aunt that Marie learns the skills of hospitality that are to make her home in Pakistan in later years a haven for so many people. Aunt Ida shows her how to run a house with Swedish neatness and order. Linens are starched and ironed. The house is never without flowers. This is Marie's particular responsibility while she stays with them.

The house always seems full but the boys, four of them, and

the two girls, as well as the men-folk, know well who is in charge, who makes the rules for the house and keeps everything flowing smoothly. Meals are communal. The meal will not start until all are seated and then the blessing is asked. If one is late, all wait.

Marie is learning valuable lessons that will guide her on her return to Ronan and throughout her later life. They are part of a Swedish community living an ordered Nordic life. Many others of the Swedes also have orchards and the sons help the fathers before and after school and through the holidays. The daughters have their roles assisting the mother in the house. Each mother takes seriously the duty of training the next generation of girl to be a good cook, a good seamstress, a good homemaker and a good wife. The girl might go on to be a teacher or a nurse but these are essential skills every woman will need to fulfill her role in life.

Uncle Charlie and Aunt Ida are founding members of the Swedish Evangelical Covenant church in Selah. Their lives, and the lives of the children, are inevitably largely focused on the Covenant church activities. They use Swedish Bibles. The sermons are in Swedish. Eventually the youth activities, and there are many, lead the way in the slow change from Swedish to the American vernacular.

Marie's four high school years are spent back in northern Montana being helpmeet to her father and a substitute mother to her brother until he leaves home after high school midway through her time there. They live on the Flathead Indian Reservation under the shadow of the Mission range of the Rocky Mountains. Ronan, the nearest town, is a few miles south of Flathead Lake.

Marie recollects watching from the farm Indians herding their buffaloes along the traditional trails north toward the lake—and remembers the bitter cold of winter and the horse drawn wagon on skids over snow to school.

Study comes naturally. She enjoys it and has an ability to lock out distractions. She has a high degree of self-discipline coupled with an inquiring perceptive mind and a retentive memory. Marie graduates from high school near the top of her graduating class as salutatorian. Throughout her life she is to show high scholastic aptitude. At nursing school and then, much later, at missionary language school she is also at, or close to, the head of her class.

Once high school graduation is over, she loses no time in moving back to central Washington. That is where her closest friends are. Her intent is to follow in Lillian's footsteps and study at the nursing school of St Elizabeth's, a large Catholic hospital in Yakima, several miles down-river from Selah.

This time the homestead in Ronan is sold up. Sam, her father, moves along with her to be with his older brother. It is the time of the Depression. Times are very difficult and families draw closer together. Even the nursing school has to give the student nurses their stipends in the form of study books. Although there is very little money for the students they are all receiving something of much greater value—spiritual example and teaching, physical and spiritual discipline, close supervision and challenging study with long hours of work. The nuns are strict and the students' hours of freedom very limited. It is an ideal training environment for a girl like Marie and she thrives on it. The example of women following a religious vocation with such devotion and joy she is never to forget.

Hospital Train in North Africa

Marie graduates as a nurse in 1935. She is just twenty-one. She is pretty and has a high sense of fun. The young men like her and there are several she likes in return. The world lies before her. She begins working in the district nurse service in her own town now that her studies are over and she is qualified. She is also considering her future. What does she want to do with her life?

During the years, desire has been slowly forming in Marie's heart and mind to become a missionary with her own Swedish Covenant Mission in inland China. This crystallizes into intention, but before she can move ahead tensions in Europe over-spill. Germany invades Poland.

When war breaks out in Europe in early September 1939, she immediately volunteers for the American Red Cross which is seeking to recruit nurses.

By the time of Pearl Harbor on December 7th, 1941 she has already been in the Army more than a year, serving in Fort Lewis near Tacoma in Washington State and making friendships that will last throughout her life.

On Marie's twenty-eighth birthday at the end of July 1942, five nurses serving at Fort Lewis in Washington State receive posting orders to Camp Rucker, Alabama to join the 41st Hospital Train. They are being assigned to an Army hospital train medical unit which will have six nurses and carry several hundred patients. The unit will soon go overseas but although there are many guesses, quite where they will actually be sent no one knows.

For three of the five, selected at random with initials grouped together, the JKL's, it is a fortuitous selection. All three, Johnson, Kirkness and Lundquist are Swedish Covenant and of Scandinavian background. Their close friendship lasts throughout their lives.

At the beginning of September they start their journey going first to Alabama and Georgia on their way to an eventual landing in Casablanca in Morocco.

Overseas a turn is taking place in the tide of war in Africa.

Rommel has just launched his offensive at Alam Halfa in Egypt, seventy miles west of Alexandria. So close to the Nile and the Canal! It is being stoutly resisted by the British 8th Army. Rommel breaks off the attack due to fuel and ammunition shortages. Six weeks later, in mid-October, the Eighth Army goes on the offensive itself at El Alamein. After twelve days bitter fighting, Rommel only has thirty-five tanks operational out of five hundred, thirty thousand men have been captured and the fighting retreat westward across Libya begins.

The following month, November, sees Operation Torch, the North Africa landings into French Morocco and Algeria by the Americans. The British First Army lands further to the east in Tunisia. The squeeze is on. Both German and Italian troops are poured in from Italy to try to stabilize the situation. Fighting is bitter.

By early February, Rommel is defending the Mareth Line in Tunisia. To the west is the U.S. Second Corps. By April '43, the Eighth Army has cracked the Mareth line and joins up with Allied troops in Tunisia.

That same month the SS Mariposa, a troopship, docks at Casablanca on the Atlantic coast of French Morocco after eight days unescorted travel from New York. The day before the ship docks the final assault on Tunis and Bizerta has begun. In two weeks the cities will have fallen and the bulk of Axis resistance in Africa will be over.

It is a very late Easter this year. Marie, Lundy and Kirk are able to attend the services at the Allies Club in Casablanca.

(A tiny diary the size of a credit card records Marie's war and is excerpted at intervals below. It begins with her time in Morocco and Algeria.)

April 24

Disembarked at Casablanca.

They are soon at work on the 41st Hospital train. The six

women quickly sort out their congested living arrangements and routines. It means a pair of nurses sharing a compartment six feet by seven feet with hardly room apart from the bunks to hang up underwear to dry. Marie and Lundy are paired.

Over a period of more than two years in such close proximity, neither can remember a cross word between them. Lundy is younger than Marie, so when Marie eventually becomes chief nurse she feels herself to be Lundy's chaperone. When Lundy begins to date a quite unsuitable man, Marie lets her know quite firmly her opinion. That is the only time they differed that Lundy can recall.

There is a small separate latrine and a very small day room shared with the male officers that is too small to serve as a dining room. Room on board is so limited that most of the recreation and exercise has to be found outside when the train is stationary. Through the generosity of the railroad battalions, the nurses are able to have showers. An allotted time is set aside during which the unit showers are available only to the nurses. A private latrine for the nurses is also set up in the railroad yards.

Although the trains carry on average 265 patients and sometimes up to 350, each nurse is assigned one litter car of thirty beds. There are only six litter cars; the remaining cars carry walking patients. The nurse is responsible for the car in its entirety. This means supervision of the enlisted personnel, cleanliness and upkeep of the car, care of patients including administration of medicines, diet and obtaining for the patient the utmost physical and mental comfort.

Marie in addition is assigned as surgical nurse which includes supervision of the small operating / first aid room and assisting the surgical officer. On a 28-hour overnight journey each nurse will work 19 or 20 hours.

Morale is always high on the 41st H.T.

May 24

Made our first trip to Oran. (Made seven trips, about eight thousand miles, to Oran.)

There is eventually a rail network of twelve hundred miles along the North Africa coast from Casablanca to Bizerta. Three of the locomotives, 2–8–0's, in the Military Transportation Service have been shipped over from the States but most of the rolling stock in North Africa is French. The engineers and staff of the MTS are almost all railroad men from home.

In June Marie writes a letter home telling about railroad life.

The train is made up of French cars so you can be sure it isn't the latest in trains. It isn't too bad, tho.' We have seen worse in our African travels. In fact this train is known as the best hospital train in North Africa – it would be. The patients are brought to us on stretchers which are hung three deep on racks on each side of the cars. These ward cars resemble boxcars more than anything else – except they have windows in them. When the old train gets up a little speed the stretchers swing and sway until I don't see how the boys stand it but they aren't the kind to complain.

Besides the ward cars we have a pharmacy car with blood plasma, IV solution of all kinds and just everything a good hospital needs. We have a supply car and a kitchen car with wood stoves. The cooks really take it on the chin working in that hot kitchen.

Our quarters are compartments – French style – really quite comfortable but not to be confused with the American variety. We don't see any hot water from the time we leave our home base until we get back which is usually about a week. On the trip our helmets serve as our bathtubs. It is quite a trick to stand on one foot with the other in a helmet of water on a rocking train. Even at our home base these helmets serve as our washbasins and wash tubs.

All in all we like our job and wouldn't trade with anyone except possibly the girls in advanced surgical units. We are evacuating the casualties from the last big battles now. About half of every load is German prisoners. The army is bending over backwards to observe the Geneva Convention so these boys are treated just like our own. It seems to be true that the Germans are doing their part in observing the Red Cross so we are quite safe. On one trip some weeks ago, before we were allowed to go with the train, the boys ran into two bombings but the train wasn't touched.

We go through some very picturesque and colorful mountains that remind me of Naches, Goldendale and the Ellensburg canyon. Even the mountainsides are terraced for farming. The Arabs do the most beautiful job of farming I ever expect to see. Instead of fences they have lovely hedges, rows of trees or flowers dividing their land. There are gorgeous flowers everywhere but never a weed in sight. Some still use primitive methods but now and then we see a binder or other piece of machinery. The camel and the donkey are the principal beasts of burden. They load the poor things down until you are sure they can carry not one more straw and then the owner gets on top of the load and away they go.

Last time I told you we were cold. That is all changed. It gets hotter by the hour and the flies worse by the minute. They practically eat us alive! Have I told you about our mosquito nets? Home is where we hang them now. At first we thought the nets were a nuisance but now we can't live without them, because of the flies, not the mosquitoes.

Freda, I can eat dirt with the best of them now and never flinch. At first it nearly turned my stomach upside down to see some of the markets but now nothing disturbs me. I go without a bath from one week to the other and if the water isn't hot when we get home, just take a cold shower and be glad for the water.

We eat canned rations, there are plenty of them but we are always hungry. We are rationed to four candy bars a month, which we buy and eat the first day so we don't have to worry about them any more.

Marie then expands on the details of a meal the six girls have on a U.S. Navy ship.

The Navy must have felt like the Elks club when they feed the poor children at Christmas!

June 27

Sidi Bel Abbes – Two cases of dynamite under train. One under the personnel car and one under car 14.

July 2

Several accidents on railroad. A mine was laid on the track for us just outside of Oujda.

On July 9th the invasion of Sicily begins. The hospital train continues its runs along the coast of North Africa.

July 16

A ship exploded in the harbor in Algiers while we were on the docks.

July 27

While we were between five gas tankers and an ammunition dump some gas barrels exploded.
Made three trips to Algiers before going back to Casablanca for repairs.

August 2

Left Casablanca for Meknes where train was repaired.
Met American missionaries whose home became 'a rest upon the way.'
Had tea at Cherif's and later, dinner at his home.

Marie meets with the young heir apparent who is later to become King of Morocco. Her letter captures her lively curiosity and the pleasure in encountering a different culture and customs. For the first time she is to encounter overseas missionaries at work and the memory stays with her.

This week our train was laid up for repairs in a most interesting city. Of course we continued to live on the old wreck even while the repairs were going on but regardless of that it was one of the most interesting weeks we have spent in Africa. The first day we were there the C.O. got a pass for us to visit the old walled city in which the

native Moroccans live. We hired a guide and proceeded
to see the sights.

The streets are dark, twisting, mysterious looking alleys
from which one could never find the way without a guide.
The homes are entered through low doorways in blank
walls but it is surprising what beauty one finds inside. The
shops are stalls set in the walls with everything under the
sun for sale. Just such markets as you would expect existed
centuries ago. In some of these shops we saw some material
so fine and with such exquisitely lovely designs that one
could hardly believe it was real. It seemed the sort of thing
princesses in fairy tales would wear. Even for $15 a yard
they would not sell it to us.

As we were snooping around in the Medina, as the old city
is called, a young Syrian girl who had lost her guide asked
if she might go with us until we got back to the gate. She is
a most interesting girl – a war refugee from France – and
speaks nine languages. We also found she is a Christian
with ideas like our own. Thru her everything happened to
make the week interesting.

She arranged for us to visit a palace in the city which
is occupied by an uncle of the Sultan – a charming old
gentleman. We expected only a sort of tour of the grounds
but we were asked to stay for tea. We sat on cushions on the
tile floor looking out into a tiled courtyard with a fountain
in the center. The water for the tea was heated in a brass
teakettle over a brass charcoal burner. We were served two
kinds of native cookies and three kinds of preserves. One
was made of candied orange blossom petals gathered from
their garden.

A couple of days later along came an invitation to have
dinner at the summer home of the same family in the

country. Dinner was served on the porch. Of course we sat
on the floor with many cushions to recline among between
the courses. The food came on platters which were placed on
tables about ten inches high. There were about ten courses
and everything was eaten with the fingers. The whole
roast or the whole chicken or whatever it happened to be
is placed in the center of the low table and everyone just
breaks off a piece. It isn't as messy as it sounds because there
are napkins as large as hand towels and water is passed
after eating to wash the hands. There are four or five meat
courses – delicious meat, too – a couple of vegetables and a
native dish.

After that there is a rest followed by fruit.

Then another rest followed by mint tea.

The old gentleman himself is very charming and his eyes
sparkle with mischief. He got as much fun out of having
us as we had from being there. His three sons are also
most charming. They ate with us and there was certainly
nothing stiff or formal about the affair – it came closer to
being hilarious.

They were as curious about us as we were about them.
We were able to carry on a spirited conversation thru our
Syrian friend. They asked us all about America and about
us and what we thought of the seclusion in which their
women must live. Those boys were pretty witty and we
couldn't get ahead of them too much. There was a lot of
fun and laughing at the table. The oldest son is married
to a princess whom we later met. Her clothes, and those
of her sisters-in-law, were gorgeous. We were taken to
their part of the house because they must not show their
faces when there are men other than their own immediate
family present.

We sat on cushions with them and carried on a little conversation with them through our friend. The youngest son has very modern ideas but out of deference to his father he abides by the family customs. He is majoring in mathematics at college and seemed to be a very serious minded chap. He thinks American boys get a break in being allowed to choose their own wives. He would at least like to be able to see the girl before he finds himself married to her but that can't be because all marriages are arranged by the parents. All, or rather most, of these people are very temperate. They never touch alcohol and are not supposed to smoke. One of these boys did smoke but not before his father.

Now for the most interesting of all the interesting things in our travels. We met four American women missionaries who live within that walled city. One is a Miss Signe Johnson from Minnesota. In fact she is a member of the Swedish Covenant church in that city although she is out under the North African Mission Board and not under our own. When she found out that three of us were Scandinavians and two of us Covenant girls she rushed right out to put the coffee pot on and we had a good old Swedish coffee party right there in the middle of North Africa!

The next day they took us on a picnic which was complete even to the potato salad. Oh, that home cooked food tasted good! That night we were given permission to spend the night with them. We had another coffee party with Swedish cookies and fattigman. That evening we sang all the old Swedish songs accompanied on the guitar by Miss Johnson. We had one more dinner there before we left. We felt so at home in their house that we just took off our shoes and would lie on their cool tile floor. Our train was so hot we could hardly stand it so we were doubly happy to be able to visit them. It was just like being with friends from home.

Yesterday before our train left here they came with a box of doughnuts and fattigman. I am sure this is the most enjoyable time we will spend in our travels. It really was 'a rest upon the way.'

August 10

Left for Algiers. French bomber with ten aboard just missed us and crashed in flames half a block away.

On August 16th Messina across the straits from Italy is captured to end the Sicily campaign and open up the prospect of carrying the war into Italy.

August 26

Air raid in Algiers. The train was parked on the docks.

Marie adds as an aside in her diary—

Never have so few been commanded by so many who knew so little about so much.

The Italian campaign opens on September 3rd, the fourth anniversary of the outbreak of war in Europe. During the first five days, British and Canadian infantry push a hundred miles up the Italian boot and into southern Italy. That same day Italy unconditionally surrenders.

On September 9th General Mark Clark's Fifth Army makes an amphibious assault landing south of Naples at Salerno. For some days the outcome is in doubt, as the Germans in bitter and tenacious fighting threaten to push the invaders back into the sea.

The hospital train crew and nursing staff are now anticipating a move over into Italy even while they continue their North Africa runs.

On October 1st General Mark Clark's Fifth Army enters Naples.

October 2–7

Spent first week of October in La Senia. Made last trip to Algiers October 6.

At last at the end of October orders for the move to Italy come. The train has been their home for the past six months. They might never see it again.

Hospital Train in Italy

1943 –1945

October 28, 1943

*We embarked at Mers-el-Kebir. Landed from LCD's
at Bagnolia.*

Bagnolia is on the coast north of Naples, between the two
major invasion landing beaches at Salerno and Anzio. It is Naples

that is now to be the base for the 41st Hospital train, once it gets hold of another train.

November 1

Four alerts in five days. Air raid.

November 10

Air raid early morning. Bomb dropped thirty feet from our quarters.

The bomb grazes the building in which hundreds of nurses are living but it is a dud and it is dug out of the street the following morning.

November 21

Train presented to us by General Gray.

November 22

Our first trip to Caserta.

November 25

Thanksgiving! Had dinner with Capt *Beck at 3rd Sec Mess. Had marvelous time but lost the train. Had to call railway battalion for a guide.*

November 26

At long last Frank was a patient. There aren't words for

*the occasion. Had turkey again. Finished the day by an air
raid while we were on the docks.*

November 28

*Saw Frank today. Margaret Bourke White took pictures of
our train for Life magazine. Someone threw a switch in
attempt to wreck train.*

December 9

Day off. Saw La Traviata with Capt Beck.

Marie is taking every advantage of her opportunities. When
possible Kirk, Lundy and she visit the Waldensian church and,
more particularly, the orphanage at Casa Materna to the south-
west side of Naples. Marie has always been interested in Euro-
pean history. All the girls use their off time to visit interesting
locations, sometimes with overnight journeys. There is no shortage of escorts to help Marie indulge her enjoyment of opera.

December 17

*Crossed Volturno. Went to Sparonise, twelve miles from
front, could hear guns.*

December 20

Heard opera Tosca.

December 24

Heard symphony concert at San Carlos opera house.

December 25

Christmas but worked as usual. Had turkey and trimmings. Had tea in British hospital train on next track. Heard Madame Butterfly.

January 19, 1944

Extended our run to San Riardo, can hear plenty of guns. Went to opera Rigoletto at Palm Theater.

January 21

Went to Pompeii and Sorrento.

The bitter enemy resistance considerably delays the capture of Rome which has been expected since the end of last October. Standing in the way is the heavily defended Gustav Line anchored at the town of Cassino. The hostilities become a virtual stalemate. There is a series of bloody battles into mid-December and then three further all-out attacks that fail between December and March. The last attempt involves nine hundred guns and a massive aerial bombardment yet it also fails.

Now, in January '44, in an attempt to open up the way to Rome, a further Allied landing is made at Anzio, eighty miles north of the Gustav Line and thirty-one miles south of Rome.

January 22

Invasion behind German lines. Troops crossed the Garigliano River this week. Had several days off. Got a permanent at the Red Cross. Miss Sigmon and several others killed in bombing of hospital around Anzio.

February 11

Moved to new train. Such luxury. Nobody to kick us in the face as we sleep and no hole in the bathroom floor for the icy wind to blow through.

The German counter attack at Anzio almost succeeds. By mid-February the battle has reached the final Allied defensive line. Only a valiant last-ditch stand averts the collapse of the entire Allied left flank and the certain loss of the Anzio beachhead. It has been a close run thing!

February 27

Capt Staley took us on an excursion. Saw ancient amphitheater. Heard Spellhaug was killed in bombing of hospital at Anzio.

Glenda Spellhaug is another nurse who has come with the group from Fort Lewis. She is the chief nurse of an evacuation hospital near Anzio. While walking between tents she is hit and killed by falling shrapnel. She is the first fatal casualty among the women that Marie knows well.

March 10

*After about three weeks vacation P.B.S. finally caught
up with us and we got stuck on temporary duty at 36
General, Caserta. It all came because we asked for leave
to go to Capri.*

March 11

*Ah, me! - haven't worked this hard in years. Everyone is
exhausted.*

During March, Vesuvius erupts with one of its most violent
eruptions for decades. Ash and boulders cover the track five miles
away with up to twenty inches depth and freight trains have to
stop. The hospital train inches forward with crews clearing the
track and points ahead of it.

March 23

Made a trip up Vesuvius today. A truly awesome sight.

March 24

*Arrived at Capri. Spent five days seeing things and eating
ashes from Vesuvius. Stayed at Hotel Touristico. Made a
trip around the island by launch. Climbed caves, ascended
through the Blue Grotto. Saw ruins of Tiberius' castle.*

May 2

Made a marvelous trip to Amalfi, Ravello, Salerno and

coast points. One of the most beautiful drives I have ever seen. Capt Beck and Sgt Elkins took me.

May 12

We were suddenly ordered back to the train on two hours notice. Almost had to make a trip tonight.

On May 17th '44, less than three weeks before the cross-Channel invasion, the fourth major attempt to break the Gustav Line finally succeeds. Allied preparations include the most massive build-up of artillery ever undertaken in the war. When the Polish II Corps succeeds in capturing the monastery of Monte Cassino the long sought breakthrough is at last realized and the front becomes fluid.

May 19

Went to Selasa today. Troops are advancing so fast we can't keep up. Hauling French and Arabs.

General Kesselring begins a full-scale retreat on 22 May. Next day more than a thousand guns signal the beginning of the breakout from Anzio.

The fall of Rome occurs just before the cross-Channel invasion.

June 4

Rome fell today!

June 6

Allies invaded France. Maybe we will make it home under five years now.

June 16

Since the railroad isn't complete to Rome we were sent to 300 General on Detached Service (D.S.)

July 8

Called at 9:30 am and given half an hour to pack to return to the train. Thought surely we must be leaving immediately for Rome and points north. As usual when we got to the train they weren't expecting us and the train wasn't leaving for two days. Went to orphanage in the evening.

July 9

Sunday. Went to the orphanage at Portici.

July 10

Started for Rome at 8 am. Miss Mischner is along. 8 p.m. Only at San Risido forty-five miles from Naples. There is a week ahead. It's a beautiful evening.

July 11

Still on the road to Rome. The railroad has been jammed with trains. We've made around seventy-five miles in thirty-eight hours. Spent most of the morning in the catacomb remains of what was Cassino. Even after being warned I wasn't prepared for such utter desolation. It doesn't seem possible that such destruction could be brought about by human beings. Here and there among the rubble and ruins were white crosses marking graves of our men. The destroyed abbey atop the hill, which caused so many men to die, is just a heap. One wonders for what all this sacrifice was made. As we left those ruins that are slowly being turned into swamps by the debris filled rivers I felt we were leaving a desecrated cemetery. That sight sobered me more than anything I've seen in all these months. Even the trees are dead. The destruction in that entire section is unbelievable.

July 12

Made a quick tour of Rome, spending most of the time in St Peter's, that magnificent beautiful showplace in which there is enough gold to feed all of Italy while instead the Italians go hungry.

July 17

Another trip to Rome – twenty-four hours this time with three days there – met a Capt Dryden who took me to the opera and to dinner. Even bought me a gardenia. We traveled by horse and carriage.

July 23–27

Made two trips to Battapaglia to evacuate 59 Evac.

*Hitchhiked both times fifteen miles to beach at Paestium.
Saw wreckage of Salerno invasion.*

July 28

My thirtieth birthday. Went on picnic to Sorrento.

August 15

Invasion of southern France.

August 23

*During August we made three trips to Rome. On one
Capt Staley took us on a jeep tour, on another Capt Beck
did likewise.*
*During August advances on all fronts, except Italian, were
fantastic. Plans changed unbelievably.*

December 16

HQ was suddenly moved to Leghorn's San Marco station.

December 28

*The holidays were quiet and cold but we had a good time.
Made a trip to Naples. Germans were making a push on
our sector of the front.*

January 28

I made a two-day trip to Siena. Had a grand time.

February 16

Maj Bell, Lundy and I made a trip to Florence and Sesto. During February I made many visits to Pisa and vicinity.

April 14

Had a chocolate ice cream soda at XII A.F. HQ!!!!

April 15

Went to Pisa. Had dinner with Italian colonel and his wife. Attended memorial services for the President (Roosevelt) and went to a ball game.

April 16

Two years ago today we left the States. Today made our first trip to Pistacia, Florence, Leghorn. The spring push is on.

April 28 - May 2

From Pisa to Aulina with prisoners.

May 7

THE DAY!!!! (This was the end of the war in Europe.)

May 29

Uncle Charles died.
Nurses have been living in Minerva Hotel, Florence for
some time.

June 6 - 12

Spent five wonderful days in Venice.

July 12

From Florence to Merano with prisoners of war and from
Verona to Leghorn with Americans.

July 16

To Caserta. Returned with prisoners of war.

July 19

Irv came aboard the train to tell us our orders were in.
What a stir! We managed to get off the train in Florence-
!!!! which writes finis to one big chapter of our lives.

July 23

Florence to Naples and became a member of 7th
Replac. Depot.

July 28

Thirty-first birthday. Orders came to fly to Casablanca.
Three years ago today we got our overseas orders.

Things are not yet smooth sailing, or rather, flying. In Casablanca, Lundy is left off the transatlantic flight list and is to leave on a later flight. Marie is having none of it. The wires hum and there are some confrontations. This unit travels as a unit. If one can't go they all stay! They all go.

After more than five years Army service, Marie is discharged at the beginning of 1946. Initially she goes back to Yakima and works in St Elizabeth's on the staff and also does private nursing in the town. It will not, however, be for long.

Farewell, Chicago

Summer, 1947

Marie is taking her first tentative steps towards China. She feels she needs some further education in Missions. Naturally enough, the only place for that is North Park College in Chicago, the Swedish Evangelical Covenant College. She leaves her work in Yakima without any regrets. Her friends from Selah have progressed to North Park and some are still students there.

Thirty or forty percent of the students on the North Park attendance register seem, although it may be exaggeration, to be Johnsons. At this point they switch to first names and even so have sometimes to go to both forenames, even a father's first name, to sort them out. It is a cultural feast for the students, a gathering of the youth of the Nordic Diaspora. The Scandinavian customs and festivals are celebrated with a gusto and razzmatazz that would have made their progenitors tremble.

Marie's spell there as a student is to be interrupted by dramatic events elsewhere on the world canvas. She never completes the course she is studying.

The years in the late Forties subsequent to the Second World War are full of turmoil. Colonial empires crumble. Unity created by a common enemy dissolves into internal disunity and rebellion once that common enemy is removed from the scene. A new order is emerging. The noisy and fractious United Nations will become, against all previous precedent, the enduring forum for the airing of disputes and the monitoring of peace and war and international relations.

Events in China are moving fast. Communist strength is growing and the Nationalist strength under Chiang Kai Shek waning. Captured Japanese weapons and, later, U.S. weapons seized from the Nationalists enable the capture by the Communists of vital railways and industrial centers to the north. They switch, sensing the kill, from guerrilla warfare to full-scale offensive campaigns.

The vast missionary enterprise within China is also crumbling. Whether anything will eventually remain only time will show. The doors into China are closing and missionary families are making their hurried ways towards the coastal ports as and when they can. Concern for the Swedish families in the hinterland is growing even as Marie is beginning her course.

Marie's attention, like that of the rest of the world, is also focused on events rapidly and tragically unfolding in another part of Asia, India. The British are leaving India. It is to be partitioned into three parts, the center part will remain India but the east and west sections will become the two *wings* of a new nation with an impossible geography and an Islamic ideology, Pakistan.

As the date approaches for independence of Pakistan in the middle of August 1947 millions flee their homes for safety across the desert. At the beginning of that particular day, the borderline is only surmise. By evening it is still only a line on a piece of paper but the fate of millions has been sealed. For many of those millions, the family roots of centuries into land and property, into local customs and culture, are irretrievably severed. Daily, both before and after Partition Day, there are reports of massacres as one of the greatest migrations in history takes place in a few short months. Crowded steam trains arrive at Lahore and Amritsar with no one alive on them except the driver, fireman and guard.

Church World Service puts out a desperate plea for short-term medical help. Its notice to the subscribing denominations filters down quickly through the church bureaucracies. A small notice appears on the general notice board at North Park College.

Marie's response is one of those unforgettable marks on a person's life. It is to change everything.

Marie Johnson and Horace McGuill

Departure for Karachi

November 21, 1947

Marie meets Norval and Dorothy Christy at the hotel in New York the evening before departure. She has flown in from Chicago and the Christys from Pittsburgh in Pennsylvania. They are to leave at noon the following day from La Guardia airport.

Marie takes them to dinner at a Russian restaurant in the Bowery and laughs at the wide-eyed country girl just ten years her junior. Every knife the knife-thrower throws at his living target brings a shriek of horror. Kebabs served at the table flaming on the spit are similarly treated. This promises interesting reactions when they meet reality at their destination. In the meantime, Marie discovers more about this interesting couple.

The Norval Christys, newlyweds to whom this journey is a honeymoon, are from Pennsylvania and New England. They look terribly young to be going on an assignment of this nature, surely not yet their mid-twenties. They are well informed about India and Pakistan and know the names and locations of many Punjab mission stations. Both of them have applied for appointment to the India field of their Presbyterian mission. This has now been cut in two by the boundary line between India and Pakistan along the Ravi River.

Norval is from Pittsburgh. He has grown up in a home designed to nurture the faith of the four children. The parents are committed to God and hedge in their children with prayer, counsel and credible example. Father is a credit manager for a wholesale dry goods business but his vocation lies in his relationship with God. He is a Sunday school superintendent and an elder in his United Presbyterian church. This is a small denomination with its heartland in Pennsylvania. It will later merge into the larger Presbyterian Church, U.S.A. It is a church committed to overseas missions with work in Egypt, Sudan and Ethiopia and also in India.

The parents' prayers bear fruit although it means for them costly separation from their children and from their grandchildren.

Wilbur, the oldest brother, has been a district missionary in their Indian mission, known as the Sialkot Mission, since before the war. Wayne will spend his working life in the religion department of the denomination's college in New Wilmington, Pennsylvania. Ruth will marry a Presbyterian preacher.

Norval is the youngest. At the age of fifteen he has made the decision that his life will be spent wherever God wants him to be. Not long after, months only, he knows that he wants to be a doctor. The U.S. Army finances his medical education but he is unable to serve in the army of occupation in Germany because he has been discharged from the Army with a damaged knee cartilage.

This is for Norval the hand of God. Even before he has obtained a job at Hartford, Connecticut, he applies to his church for appointment as a medical missionary, expressing a preference for the Sialkot Mission where his brother is working.

Dorothy is from Springfield, Massachusetts. She has from childhood wanted to be a nurse but things have really all come together for her during her nursing education at Hartford. A Baptist minister challenges her to commit her life to Christ and then she is further challenged to missions by one of the instructors in the nursing school who has herself been a missionary nurse in India. Dorothy is also, incidentally, falling in love with a quiet and reticent young intern from Pennsylvania who has given his life over to God and is anticipating working in India. He works on her ward in the hospital.

Norval has received a call from the mission board of his church in Philadelphia only the previous month. They are looking for short-term help with emergency medical relief for perhaps up to six months. Can he bring forward his plans to serve in the Sialkot Mission? Dorothy and he are in quick agreement. There has to be some snappy footwork, the team needs to be in India before Thanksgiving late in November. Dorothy and he are already engaged. Hurried preparations are in motion. No need to set up a house, no need to buy furnishings, how soon can they get married? What will they need to take with them and how can it be sent? All the preparations have been completed and they are ready to meet their team leader at La Guardia in the morning.

By the time the meal finishes Marie and Dorothy have become fast friends. Neither has had a sister but that evening each has found one.

They have no trouble finding Mac at the airport. He has already talked to them on the phone, answered questions about what they shall take and where they shall meet. They like him immediately. He lives locally and so there are introductions to be made to his farewell party, his mother, brothers and sisters and several friends.

Horace McGuill is a missionary on furlough. He has left India before the trouble really begins to develop. It has gone totally out of control very quickly. He is fluent in the languages they will meet. He is a natural choice to lead their group.

Mac's distinct New York accent, more purely discerned in his brothers and sisters, has been moderated and Anglicized by six years abroad. He is finding it difficult to exclude from his welcoming conversation words borrowed from India that for his listeners have as yet no meaning.

Like most other preachers he is relaxed about meeting strangers. His conversation gives frequent unforced reference to a companionship with God. He is not concerned about the uncertainties ahead of them. The news reports of the Punjab in flames disconcert him not at all. Rumors spread faster than fire. Things are quieting down now. He is spending much of the time at the airport before departure with his mother. She is reminding him to take care and that he still has a good portion of his furlough yet to come. His warm smile, easily triggered, is frequently in evidence; he is looking forward to going back and being able to help.

Mac, for his part, has been curious about his team members. He is well acquainted with Norval's brother who is a missionary in Gujranwala district. Wilbur and Marj are already good friends who have been his hosts on a number of visits south.

The Christys have each other but Mac is concerned that the fourth member of the team, recruited from Chicago but clearly from further west than that city, not feel isolated. There is no one she knows seeing her off so he makes sure she is included in the larger group and not neglected.

After they have been shepherded to the departure area he has time to take stock. She is a little shorter than he, about average height, slight build, brown luxuriant hair, lightly made up, wearing a light brown linen suit and, perched on the back of her head, a matching brown hat that frames her face. She wears light rimmed spectacles over hazel eyes. She is surprisingly composed for someone embarking on such an adventure, less excited even than himself. She is probably a little younger than he is. She looks competent, and old enough to have had useful previous nursing experience. She has a lovely smile. When she smiles it seems her whole face lights up. He is pleased to see that she has a sense of humor; she laughs easily and quickly sees the point of a joke. Mac decides with a certain relief that he is going to enjoy working with all three of them. They might well make a good team. He can't help noticing that Marie is wearing neither a wedding ring nor an engagement ring.

Others have also noticed that. Both his brother and his sister, seeing him off, look with interest at the companions who will be traveling with him. Both observe to their mother on the journey home the same thing about their bachelor brother, "You watch, Horace and Marie are going to get married."

The team study each other curiously as they pass through the airport terminal procedures and on to the plane. This journey will give them opportunity to become acquainted—it is already clear to each of them that the group is coalescing nicely and there are no problem personalities likely to make working together difficult. Although they are gathered in haste for a short assignment of a few months, a random selection, the four will prove to be inseparable until death or retirement parts them. The relief assignment for the Christys is for six months to a year. They will not return to the United States for seven years and Marie will see them off from the Punjab on retirement forty years later.

They fly to Karachi by a Constellation of American Airlines. It will stop at Gander (overnight because of engine trouble), Reyk-javik, Shannon, Amsterdam, Rome and Djeddah before pulling to its screeching halt near the great airship hangar on the outskirts of Karachi.

Let us take opportunity to learn some more about the leader of this four-strong enterprise heading into the chaos of an erupted disintegrating India.

Mac

The Preparation Years

From the American Civil War onwards there have been developing increasingly efficient methods of killing more and more people. The scale of war engagement is intensifying to a crescendo.

The Battle of Hastings in 1066 was fought with less than fifteen thousand men in combat. It not only affected the development of the Anglo-Saxon nation of Britain being ruled by French government but also the whole of Europe for centuries

In July 1914 Archduke Francis Ferdinand, heir apparent to the

Austro-Hungarian Empire, has been assassinated by a Serbian student in Sarajevo. A month later, Great Britain declares war on Germany. The war rapidly expands beyond these two countries and becomes known as the First World War.

This time marks the great divide between the centuries, between the past world and the modern world. More than a million men on each side will become ranged against each other. The casualties during the Battle of the Somme in the fall of 1916 exceed one and one quarter millions. Britain alone suffers 60,000 casualties on the first day of the battle.

There will never be any going back. A line has been drawn. The flower of Europe's youth will die in the trenches and later on American youngsters will drop beside them. The New World, whatever shape it takes, will have to be shaped by their children for they have no other part to play but their own sacrifice.

On August 2, 1914, just as the war begins, a child, a boy, is born in New York City of Irish / Swedish American parents. His parents name him Horace but to most of his later friends he will be known simply as Mac. Five days earlier a first daughter is born to Swedish immigrants in Montana. One day their paths will cross.

Mac's father is a tall handsome Irishman from Ardee in County Lough. After he comes to America he is a soldier in the US 7th Cavalry Regiment before he becomes Chief of Police, Erie Railroad, Eastern Division. His office is in Jersey City and he commutes daily from Midland Park, New Jersey, where the family lives. Mac's mother is Swedish although she was raised in Finland. She grew up in a Seventh Day Adventist home. Both her mother and father are Sunday School teachers at the local Methodist Church and family devotions and church attendance are a part of the family routine.

Horace McGuill has two sisters, Clara and Margaret, and two brothers, Maynard, older than himself and one younger, Larry. The five children are spaced at roughly two-year intervals.

As they grow into their late teens the two younger boys keep company with a group of others of like age, usually a crowded car full, who live in the loosely connected towns of Midland Park, Ridgewood, Glen Rock, Wyckoff and Hawthorne. These towns are grouped around Route 208 north of Paterson, New Jersey, about twenty miles northwest of the George Washington Bridge into New York. Horace and Larry attend the Methodist church in the morning and then walk three miles on Sunday afternoon to meet up with their friends at Hawthorne.

A natural leader of the group, Jacob, is the son of Pieter Bakker who owns the locally famous hardware store in Midland Park. Jacob has a car. Jacob and Horace have a close lifelong friendship.

Most of us, I believe, have critical *hinge experiences* upon which our subsequent lives seem to turn. One event, often unexpected, occurring in a few brief moments, triggers and creates a sequence that continues to echo throughout the years that follow. Frequently these hinge experiences occur to individuals between the ages of fifteen and twenty-five. This is natural enough. These are the years when we are moving out of puberty and becoming aware that our actions, rather than those of our parents, are going to determine what happens to us socially, educationally, religiously and emotionally.

At the age of fifteen or sixteen, while still at high school, Horace has such an experience. It is to change his life forever. It starts innocently enough with a couple of adventurous friends going into the woods off Wyckoff Avenue to fire pot shots with an old revolver one of them has got his hands on. The gun discharges unexpectedly and Horace is shot in the abdomen. He limps out of the woods half a mile to a friend's house and is rushed to Paterson General Hospital. His intestines are punctured and the bullet is lodged next to his spine.

The doctors give little encouragement. Larry recalls later:

> *My dad got down on his knees in the corridor of the hospital and promised the Lord that if the boy lived he would give him to the Lord's work and put him through school to equip him to do it.*
>
> *I saw the change in my brother's life from here on in. He came to grips with the important issues of life and determined to live for Christ. He became one of the most spiritual men I have ever known. I know the change in his life style was genuine. He proved it many times.*

Horace finishes his high school at Central High in Paterson. His mother wants to make a farmer out of him and he takes the agricultural course there. It doesn't work, he isn't cut out to be a farmer, but he does finish high school.

Larry writes

> *He was a very dedicated person. He was the kind of spiritual person my father accepted. His shoes were never shiny, his knees were baggy, his pants were never pressed, his tie was askew and he had a Bible under his arm and a far-away look in his eyes. That suited my Dad's picture. Horace's personality was very studious, very quiet, very reserved and deeply spiritual.*

Mac's guide verse that he quotes on several occasions appears to have been Joshua 1:9

> *Have not I commanded thee?*
> *be strong and of a good courage;*
> *be not afraid neither be thou dismayed:*
> *for the Lord thy God is with thee whithersoever thou goest.*

The unifying factor for many of the committed young Christian people in that area of New Jersey in the early thirties is the ministry of an outstanding pastor, Hermann Braunlin.

The pastor of Madison Avenue Baptist Church, Paterson in the late Twenties sends his keen young Sunday School assistant, an accountant, to take care of a Bible class that meets at the Fire Station at nearby Hawthorne. That Bible class grows into Hawthorne Gospel Church and Hermann, giving up his accountancy, is to have a sixty-four year ministry with that one church. Brother Larry will eventually become his associate in that work.

Hawthorne becomes and still is one of the most effective and influential churches on the eastern seaboard. In its group for teenagers, the two youngest McGuills find a vitality, a warmth and a challenge they have never before experienced.

Something of deep spiritual significance happens in January 1934 during a Mission at Hawthorne led by two remarkable women. Mac makes a private transaction with God that seals his fate and future. He feels God has separated him unto Himself. From now on his directions are one way only—a closer walk with God and God's Will for his life.

In the mid 1930's while Hitler's Germany is flexing its muscles for war, Hawthorne is exerting an immense appeal to serious minded young men and women who seek a Way of peace. The vitality of that community of young people, well led and nurtured, is to propel hundreds of young people over the years into full time Christian work. Mac is just one of them and Hawthorne is the church that will support him throughout his missionary life.

In the mid-thirties a remarkable ninety to a hundred young people from the Friday night Bible class of the Hawthorne Gospel Church are attending Moody Bible Institute in Chicago, eight hundred miles to the west. Among them is Horace McGuill. God has a purpose for his life and he is determined to find it.

Mac at Moody

Moody Bible Institute (MBI) in Chicago, founded by the nine-teenth century's great evangelist D.L. Moody, is considered by many, and not only by its alumni, as the outstanding school in the world as far as practical Christian training is concerned. Moody graduates supplied and still supply many members of the task force of Christian workers around the world.

Horace's father keeps his promise. In 1934, he sends his son off to the Moody Bible Institute. The young man enrolls in the three-year pastor's course and enjoys this educational venture away from home. He is just twenty, enjoying life and full of enthusiasm. He writes back about how wonderful it is to be in a Christian atmosphere enjoying the fellowship and training for the Lord's work. A year later Larry follows him there.

While his two younger sons are at Moody, Father is baptized in believer's baptism in Paterson, New Jersey. Later his wife will follow him. We see, as we shall later see in others also, the profound influence godly parents have in the lives of their children. It is said glibly that behind every great man stands a great woman. We might as fairly say that behind most great men and women of God are parents on their knees. This is certainly so with the McGuill family.

Dad helps both boys through MBI with regular checks from home on which the boys rely. While Mac is at Moody he begins to keep an occasional journal where he notes events and adds candid observations about others and about himself. Written in a precise and clear hand, they begin at the end of August 1935, when he is commencing his second year. At this time he is just twenty-one. The journals continue intermittently until December 11, 1939.

Read in the light of his tragically short life, the journals trace the development of a young man's passion for Christ.

Sunday Sept 8, 1935

Jacob tells me that he puts in his journal just plain facts. My journal seems more for the purpose of putting down thoughts than facts.

One of the thoughts has to do with young ladies. My position I find to be a peculiar one. Since my Christian life began I have not been going with any girl as most of my friends seem to be doing. If the plain unvarnished truth were to be told I was attracted to Wilma Anderson though I fooled myself for a while into thinking I only associated with her for her spiritual development. Now she means little to me although I still pray for her growth in grace. In my third term back at Moody I seemed attracted to Andrea Barton, a nice girl but not exceptionally spiritual, but that only lasted for a very brief time, perhaps a month.

It does strike me as being strange that I should not be as natural as others in my relation to the young ladies. I am attracted to them as a whole but no particular one has ever interested me for long. Larry's oft repeated statement is that when I do fall I will fall hard. And that is the way it should be, I think.

Thursday October 3, 1935

It seems as though I am not as immune to sentimental shallow states of mind (or heart) as I thought I was. The object of my fancy has been the girl who substituted in Miss Carlson's place as nurse. I hesitate to admit it but one of the first things I noticed was that she was wearing no ring. She isn't particularly good looking but she seemed attractive in the nurse's uniform as I lay in bed. This case didn't last long, just one week.

Saturday October 5, 1935

I discover about myself that I am at first too coldly critical of a young lady but after I get to know her I allow her good qualities overcome her lack in appearance. I seem to size up a girl as some people size up a hat – 'how does this look with me?' Pride fosters such an attitude and pride is the condemnation of the devil.
I must turn my eyes from myself to God. He is the Maker of men and He has been turning out some good workmanship where the material was yielded to His skillful hands.

Thursday October 15, 1935

In my interview with Dr. Fitzwalter I asked him about finishing Moody, college and seminary. Recognizing that the Methodist machine was a hierarchy he advised nevertheless that I attend a sound Methodist college, perhaps Asbury in Kentucky or Taylor in Indiana, after I completed the pastor's course here.

A journal entry in the New Year gives a first indication that he might be interested in a different vocation *in the Lord's work* than that of pastor:

January 23, 1936

I attended the Mohammedan Prayer Band today and was convicted of the great need of countless souls who have not heard the gospel of the grace of God. Not only among the Moslems but also in all the far corners of the earth. I am thankful that I never received a definite call to the pastorate because now I am still a possible candidate for the mission field. God make me strong in Thy strength to battle for Thee.

Saturday February 1, 1936

Now here is a secret. I am almost afraid to put it in. If ever I was close to falling in love it's now. But the young lady deserves a far better person than myself. She is a wonderful Christian, known and respected by everyone. But this emotion has only come over me a few days. I'll wait and see how the Lord leads.

Thursday February 6, 1936

The questions I used to ask Jimmy are being answered for me now by my own experience. With a little encouragement I think I'll be in love.

Saturday February 8, 1936

Since January 31, when the fact suddenly dawned on me,

I have been in the grip of the strongest emotion of its kind I have ever experienced. I refer to my feelings towards the young lady and I want to analyze this. I am not sure it is love though it must be akin to it. It differs from any other attraction I've felt in its intensity and in its very nature. The doubt *is what hurts so much.*

I know, as I know that the living God answers prayer, that if I am to associate intimately with any young lady it will be under God's direction.

But is this answer to prayers for guidance the right one? If it is I thank God for choosing such a wonderful spiritual girl. If it isn't I still thank God because He knows best and He is Sovereign. Whichever way God will have it I am reconciled to that.

But, oh, how much agony there is in this suspense! That is the human element entering in and I must wait upon God. There are many things I could say after the flesh, things which all lovers in the past have said before me - why repeat? This is no child's play - I'm up against something deep and strong and which is not easily understood.

Now here is where complications have set in: during the early stages of the Conference I asked God to show me, if it was His Will, to show me in this manner, by a definite sign (the terms of which I stipulated) whether or not she is the one for me. It would take God to bring about the conditions for which I asked and I am fully persuaded that He is able.

But does He will to do it?

That's where Satan throws all sorts of things at me.

One thing about the whole matter that I like is that it is taking the pride out of me. God be thanked for that! May the whole strange business work out to His glory alone.

Sunday February 9, 1936

I sang in the choir during the evening service of the Conference. She was not there; my sign from the Lord did not come. But thank God that inner anguish is gone and replaced by a desperate trust in Jesus. The past few days I have been determinedly singing to myself 'Lean on His Arms.' Praise God for the everlasting Arms. He has borne me through the fiercest testing I've had in a long while and the result has been a closer walk with Him. Oh, how grateful I should be for everything that draws me to Him!

Mac anguishes over this young woman many days. He is unashamedly, but only in his journal, deeply in love. He is grateful his roommate has no hint of his inner turmoil. The depth of his emotions, a true first love, surprises him. He is recognizing and resolving a conflict within himself. If His Heavenly Father does not agree with his own desires then he is wholly God's to do with as He pleases. It is a seesaw experience. At times it seems as though God is favoring his courting but then her responses seem to be less than positive. His own reactions are *a desperate trust in Jesus.*

It is when I realize my utter helplessness and cast myself entirely and unreservedly upon Him that I am strengthened and blessed.

It is at this time of inner turmoil that he also talks with Dr. Hockman about missionary fields. Directions are becoming increasingly clear. What is claiming his heart and affections is Christ's call to labor in a Muslim missionary field and initially, he realizes, that is likely to be alone, whatever may ensue later.

Wednesday February 19, 1936

This whole experience has taught me some great lessons:
1. God's Will is infinitely best, don't question His wisdom in the matter.
2. I have nothing in me to justify even the least bit of pride. (What brings about these valleys of despair is the comparison between her and myself.)
3. All is not done in prayer and passive resignation but God-directed *activity has a definite place. So then Dr. Fitzwater's admonition to have the faith of a Calvinist but work like an Arminian is evidently in order.*

Saturday March 21, 1936

Sometime around the first of the year I began to read the Bible from Genesis right through. Today I reached its end.

Thursday March 26, 1936

In the Prayer Band today the request was made to pray for men to work among the Moslems. Oh, for the privilege of carrying the glad tidings to that people!

Horace is acquiring many duties, he is chairman of Prayer Bands (sub-groupings of specific Missions interests) at Moody, teaches a class of Sunday School teachers in a black church. He is a teacher at Courier Sunday School and becomes its superintendent. He leads the singing at many of the services in local churches he attends and works in a Sunday evening Young People's Fellowship. At the same time, there is a growing depth to his spiritual life and he is seeing his love for Grace and her response best left entirely in God's Hands. What He wants must prevail.

Friday May 8, 1936

I question tonight what interest the Mission Field has for me. Is it the romance, the adventure? Surely my love for souls is at a very, very low ebb. Compassionless am I. O how can one who passionately loves his God so have so little love for lost souls? But is not everything from Thee? Therefore, my Father, my faith looks up to Thee.

Tuesday May 12, 1936

This whole business of being in love can get rather tiresome - especially when the investment pays no dividends!
I have been contemplating the wisdom of changing to the missionary course in the Fall. 'Guide me, O Thou great Jehovah.'

Thursday May 14, 1936

Captain Mallis spoke for the first part of Missions Hour and spoke again after dinner to the Moslem Prayer Band. He told me of a Mission Board that is trying to place the Gospel in Afghanistan. He promised to send me the address of the board so that I may get some information. There is a strong desire to apply to that board but I will have to wait until I find out more about it.

Tuesday May 19, 1936

I was told by Dr. Hackman that Afghanistan was not to be considered as a mission field because of the treachery of the tribesmen, the policy of the government and a few other things. Well, if God will open the door then no man will shut it.

Wednesday May 20, 1936

I wrote to Dad telling him of my desire to go to labor in Afghanistan.

Thursday June 11, 1936

I may be losing a chapter of my life and opening a new one. Mr. Goedin has pointed out that which I have slowly been coming to realize, namely that this school (Moody) is turning out men of a certain mold – in mass production – and I am being cast in that mold with all spontaneity, originality and proclivities deadened and dormant. That was the sum total of his indictment with which I had to agree. I rebelled against this process, determining that this thing shall not come to pass.

The steps he advised to overcome are these – a wide background of reading, particularly biographies, a time at Wheaton (half a year or more) and then seminary at Princeton. Princeton he considers as absolutely essential for me. I was enthused and jubilant – I shall pray much. And now I look forward to the renaissance of Horace McGuill.

The Renaissance of Horace McGuill

Friday June 19, 1936

*This is a queer way for a 'renaissance' to begin – I feel a
great deal more like the Dark Ages. Beyond the shadow of
a doubt I am in a bad way physically, mentally, morally
and spiritually. If ever things were black it is right now.
Well, so much the better. I am learning to rest in God
even in the face of the most galling thing of all – my own
weakness and failure.*

Saturday July 11, 1936

*I have resigned from the chairmanship of the Prayer Bands
and from all active part in the recreation Club. I feel this is
the Lord's Will this way – I have been blessed since acting
on my decisions. My earnest desire is to abandon myself
to Jesus Christ, willingly and freely. I must be 'in Christ'
moment by moment.*

Monday July 27, 1936

*I believe that a fellow may practice the presence of God by
starting the day in the consciousness of His Presence and*

*determining, by His grace, that the moment he realizes
he cannot feel God near him he will immediately cease
everything until the fellowship is restored or the reason for
the cessation is revealed. With the help of God I want to
put this truth into action in my life.*

Thursday September 17, 1936

*Afghanistan is open! The Lord told me so, tonight.
Tomorrow I am to go to Mr. Bach at the Scandinavian
Alliance Mission (SAM) and tell him God ordered me to
come to him. Great exultation!*

Friday September 18, 1936

*Mr. Bach is out on deputation. I have a blank ready to
apply to the Scandinavian Alliance Mission.*

Horace summons up his courage and, on a walk with Grace,
informs her in a simple statement "I am completely in love with
you."

Mr. Bach, when Horace does meet him, is able to give no
encouragement about Afghanistan. The young man is also
slowly realizing that training to be a missionary will require a
long and testing period of academic training and it will require
much patience.

Monday October 26, 1936

*I used to wonder whether a fellow could be with his girl
friend and still be conscious of the Lord's presence. Well,
today as we played chess I would look at her as she was*

studying the board and my heart would go out to her in love, I love her so. Then I would lift my heart to my Lord and He sanctified my love for her. His wonderful fellowship made everything complete. Is it any wonder I am deeply happy?

Saturday November 21, 1936

My call to Afghanistan seems more sure than ever and I feel encouraged to speak very definitely to Grace tomorrow night.

Sunday November 22, 1936

I spoke to Grace tonight about my love for her and my wish that she be my co-laborer through life. I told her that under God I offered her everything I had - wanted her - needed her.
Her reply was the same as before, with a depth of feeling. She cannot give me an answer until she has more definite guidance from God. On walking home from the 'L' she placed her hand in my arm.

Saturday November 28, 1936

As I write it seems more definite than ever that I am being pointed towards Afghanistan. Faith is necessary because others have felt led there and are still outside. Many, it is said, are waiting on the Persian border. Others have thought of attempting entrance through the Khyber Pass on the eastern border but later thought better of it.

Apparently missionaries have not received a very warm reception there.

Grace leaves Moody at Christmas and goes to work in Camp Oak Hills, a Christian camp in Minnesota. They correspond.

Friday January 22, 1937

It was brought to my attention that I cannot enter college, not having had any languages in High School. This of course goes for seminary, too. Medical training is out of the question (the usual M.D. course at any rate). With these doors shut it narrows the immediate field for me. It looks as though the Missionary Medical course here at Moody or at National Bible Institute (NBI) in N.Y.C. are the only things left. Fine, that's all the sooner I'll reach the field, Lord willing and if the Lord tarry.

May 29, 1937

A young Indian was cruelly killed, butchered for preaching the Gospel in Mexico. Later his widowed wife is told that the next morning she can go and preach - her face lights up. She goes to the very town where her husband was killed and preaches the Gospel to his murderers in the power of the Holy Spirit. No cheap cross for her. For a long time he preached in Nicaragua but not once without being stoned. 'But what is that?' he said. A broken heart for sinners. When you stop bleeding you stop blessing!
Now a few thoughts of my own. What other life is worthwhile than the life wholly given to God? Mr. De Roos owns no property besides a couple of suitcases,

> *nothing but the clothes on his back. He prayed for 5000*
> *New Testaments – told no one, made no plea, organized no*
> *campaign. He got them. Then 10,000, then 15,000, then*
> *20,000. Each time he got them, through prayer.*

Horace nears the completion of his pastor's course at Moody. Wheaton College in Chicago does not accept him for enrolment; Grace gives no encouragement and, after an earlier written expression of love, speaks only of friendship.

A few days after his twenty-third birthday, he is through the pastor's course for which he enrolled in Moody. He decides to continue there and take the missionary course and will return in the fall.

Dad has come down for the graduation and they travel back together to New Jersey.

A Three-Cent Stamp

Horace spends the summer of 1937 home in New Jersey but is glad to resume at Moody in September on a course more suited to his changed needs. The years at Moody have changed him. He has become more introspective. His preferred time is spent not with his friends but with God in prayer and reflection. His devotional life deepens. His goals have clearly focused on a virtually impossible assignment. Since his first awareness of the needs of Muslim countries he has seen no other area for his endeavors. He is not looking for the hardest hill to climb but rather is willing to climb any hill God places before him, however steep it may prove to be. He is ever conscious of his own weakness and fallibility but believes God can and will enable.

A possibility of taking an opening in a boys' hostel in either Morocco or Egypt has been pushed aside under God's constraining Hand in favor of the closed country of Afghanistan. Everything points against this being a feasible commitment of his life. There are no known missionary societies working in Afghanistan and those that would work there cannot.

In his mind constantly and requiring resolution is his relationship with Grace. He loves her devotedly and his love grows. How does she feel about him and, just as importantly, how does she feel about becoming his lifetime partner and coworker in the thankless and perhaps impossible task to which God is insistently calling him?

Sunday September 17, 1937

Grace did come to Boonton on Labor Day and I spent the afternoon with her. We went up the 'Tarn' and talked quite freely about what was on our hearts. That afternoon remains in my memory as one of the most beautiful and rare days of my whole life.

Then I came to MBI again and took up my missionary studies. Grace was in Chicago three days but somehow our talks were not the same and I had an uneasy feeling. Sad, too - a little bit -, I love her more than ever, only to see her go back without knowing she loves me.

Last Monday I appeared before the Board of Directors of the Scandinavian Alliance Mission (SAM) and Wednesday I received word that I had been accepted as a candidate for India!

Monday September 20, 1937

Tonight I had planned on attending the prayer meeting at the Scandinavian Alliance Mission. I didn't have a cent for carfare, asked the Lord to supply it, He didn't, so I am in my room, planning to have a season of prayer after this entry in my diary.

Tuesday September 21, 1937

Last night I was unable to mail my letter to Grace because I had no stamp and no money and I will not borrow, not even a stamp. I asked the Lord for a three-cent stamp so that I could mail the letter that was already a day late. I arose from prayer, dismissed the matter from my mind and commenced to study.

Red Walker knocked on my door within a few minutes and asked if I had any picture wire. I gave him what I had and he offered to pay me a nickel. I, as a matter of course, refused the offer and he left. Then I remembered my need and my prayer so I thanked God for the quick answer and asked forgiveness for my blindness and prayed again for a three-cent stamp.

Wednesday September 22, 1937

I prayed again this morning for a three-cent stamp and for five cents to telephone for a necessary appointment with Mr. Bach. A student stopped me in the post office and paid me a dime which he had borrowed so I posted the letter and made the telephone call.

Mr. Bach arranged for me to see him at three this afternoon, so I was there. I walked both ways for lack of carfare and was good and tired before reaching school again. But I was glad I walked because I passed out a few tracts and had a fine talk with an intelligent Jewish lady whose bag I offered to carry.

Our discussion revealed that all things are not as I would like them - mainly, my work will not be exclusively among Moslems and so I'll probably receive little specific training for this work. Afghanistan was not mentioned at all. I am trusting everything in God's hands, nothing doubting. Mr. Bach advised me to learn to play some musical instrument and also to learn typing.

September 24, 1937

I was thinking of Grace and the uncertainty of our relationship. I headed for the stone pier where we had talked a week before. A man was fishing there. It began raining. I headed back and sat under a locust tree (my juniper tree that day). Breaking into my reverie was a scene of remarkable beauty. I was gazing idly at the lake when a transformation came over it as I watched. I was facing east. The light from behind me, shining brighter through the thinning clouds, transformed the water into a soft velvet green lawn, indescribably rich in color, softening as it met the horizon and blending exquisitely with the luminous violet glow of the storm clouds. The long Navy pier was a soft purple, its towers suggestive of faraway seaports, an unobtrusive landmark on that broad sweep of water.

Never has any scenery so impressed itself upon me as I watched God display His handiwork. My troubled thoughts had 'folded their tents like the Arabs and silently stole away.' My soul was refreshed. The lesson? I came to know that what I can't see in the future, God can see and does order. When these times of slight trial and momentary doubts come may I remember the lesson of this afternoon when God brought me out to see the constantly changing canvas of the Master-artist. There are yet more lovely things ahead, Praise His Name!

Follow on, McGuill; for good or ill, pain or pleasure – follow unquestioningly, resolutely and He will give joy in service; above all you will be serving the Great God of Wonders and the greatest Man who ever lived – Jesus Christ, the captain of our salvation who never asks you to

*go where He has not been or to be tempted where He was
not tempted or suffer what He has not suffered. My Lord
and my God!*

Horace is only a couple of months into his missionary course
when, to his surprise, he receives a direction that seems at variance
with God's previously clearly indicated purposes and design for
his life. Horace quotes first in the entry summarizing the past few
days a number of Bible promises and then continues:

Tuesday November 16, 1937

*The Scripture verses are the verses the Lord gave me that
night in prayer to corroborate the leading that came very
suddenly to me – I was to leave school!*
*The situation was interesting. I had a notebook to turn
in and an exam to take the following morning and I was
prepared for neither one. At half past nine in the evening
I thought to commence studying but as I knelt to pray for
physical and mental strength and refreshing I tarried in
prayer and soon lost all concern for studies. His voice, oh
so tenderly and softly, came to me – 'Wilt thou trust me,
child?' I considered and answered, 'Yes, Lord.' Then came
the startling leading confirmed by Scripture verses and
then borne out by circumstances. I came to see it to be a
clear case of God's having made everything in readiness for
me to step out by faith.*
*Miss Trumbull already knew, from the Lord, that I was
to leave.*

A week later Horace is still clear he has to leave but does not
know where he is to be going!

> *Marvelously a way opened up to motor south to Florida, a*
> *driver being needed. I hadn't a cent when my call came but*
> *through Cedar and others I had enough to start off with.*

Horace is not yet through with academic learning although he is through with Moody. In Florida he works with Christian friends in encouraging enrollment in a Scripture memorizing program for schools. Various other activities including frequent preaching opportunities develop.

A letter from Grace around Thanksgiving suggests that because of her own uncertainties they take a trial break from correspondence for two months. It promises to be a hard winter of waiting.

Making Connections

Horace's last journal, the fifth in the sequence, begins after mid-summer 1938, a lapse of seven months. Horace is back home in New Jersey. It seems from indirect references that he might have spent the spring / summer semester at Wheaton College in Chicago.

He is working to bring in some income but largely at loose ends while trying to determine whether attending the Missionary Medical course at the National Bible Institute in New York is in God's Will for him. He is resting entirely in God for the next move. His attempt to be a door-to-door salesman of *The Book of Life* soon convinces him he has no capacity in that direction.

Attached to one of the pages of this last journal by a rusted paper clip is a photograph of passport size. Curiosity about this young woman for whom there are hardly enough words of praise in Horace's vocabulary is somewhat assuaged by this picture of Grace. She wears a dark dress with a large white crocheted collar. Her hair is permed and close to the head. She has piercing deep-set eyes in an oval face. She wears little or no makeup. The picture captures a woman with inner strength and spiritual tranquility, a woman of beauty rather than a *pretty* woman, a woman at peace with herself, a woman it would be easy to love.

Wednesday July 6, 1938

In prayer I realized what the real way of working for God is. It is undoubtedly in sacrificial, earnest, persistent prayer. This is the way of the Spirit. The way of the world is to do, do, do.
Clara will invite Grace to stay for a visit this fall.

Wednesday August 31, 1938

Her visit to Clara's is over. We were together quite a bit and had frequent times of prayer and discussion. We spoke of the advisability of restraint from too many embraces, but with her near me I could only restrain myself with some difficulty. I do not want passion to gain the upper hand.
There was a sweet consciousness – with her and apart from her – of having struggled in prayer (alone) and having yielded all decision to Christ and thus gained victory. The way is not clear for marriage – so we do not know definitely that we are to serve God together. I rejoiced in God that I could truly say 'Thy Will be done.'
However, feeling the need of letting the family know that we only wait for conditions to open up for our marriage (this of course resting with God) we had a dinner and announced to the assembled relatives that we were 'sort of' announcing our engagement. Much joy there was in that!
Searching earnestly through the seventh chapter of I Corinthians this morning I concluded that Paul's advice – his personal advice – was to remain unmarried – the single man having more singleness of purpose serving God. But marriage is honorable and good and there is no command

forbidding it. He seems to conclude that every man should abide as he is called – single or married – every man has his calling from God.

Grace has returned to Oak Hill Christian Camp in Minnesota. Horace seems in the limbo waiting for God. He recognizes it is at least two years before he will be ready to go to India and the urgency to be doing something to advance his departure bears upon him.

Tuesday September 28, 1938

Today was a day of many questions. Some I jot down:
- *When will I be practical in matters of training?*
- *Is it right for me to turn down study at NBI for an indefinite wait?*
- *If I don't finish my training now, when will I get to the field?*
- *What certainty do I have for the future if I do not take steps to prepare for it?*
- *What will Grace say and when can we be married?*
- *Is not my guidance vague and indefinite?*
- *Could I not do better by using my own judgment in these matters?*

More than my desire to serve in Afghanistan, more than my desire for Grace, I long for God to work in my life entirely according to His pleasure. So I must wait for His voice – and when I hear it I must obey though the way be dark for me.

Wednesday October 18, 1938

In prayer this morning I considered the Raymond Lull
Home in Morocco as a possible station for me, God willing.
I hate to think, in a way, of not going to Afghanistan.

In reality I am a washout as far as missionary training
goes. I am inclined to be neglectful of details, I have
not known very much of hard work, I have no medical
preparation, no college credit to speak of – nothing, in fact,
that would recommend me to a mission board except my
Bible School training and a little experience.

But it is God who led me to Florida from my missionary
studies at MBI and it is God who kept me from the
missionary medical course at NBI – so it is God who
is directing me to a definite service. Lead on, O King
Eternal!

As soon as Christmas and the New Year celebrations are over
Horace goes to Minnesota to see Grace.

Monday January 9, 1939

The trip to Bemidge was accomplished with great
anticipation and at last I arrived and was with her. She
was as lovely as ever, and I had great spiritual blessing
and much pleasure in her presence.

But it was clear that all was not well. I did not say anything,
waiting for her to speak. On my last evening with her she
spoke but spoke with such sorrow and tenderness and in
tears. I felt no sting at the statement she made – my one
desire then was to comfort her in her evident sorrow.

The lack of response on her part was explained. She said

she would need a lot more love for me - those are her words.
I did not question. I quietly accepted and offered to do what
she thought best, whatever that be.

She drove me to the bus and when we prayed she again
cried. Then she smiled at me through her tears and said 'You
have God!' - meaning my comfort in Him. So honest and
brave and tender is she, every memory of her is precious.

Sunday morning, in Chicago, while I was reading in
Ezekiel, the burden of my sorrow miraculously lifted and I
had victory. I thanked God for it and asked Him to build
our love from these ruins and build it entirely according to
His will. For I felt sure Grace and I would yet be one.

Horace hears that there are mission stations opening on the
borders of Afghanistan but that the borders to the country itself
are resolutely closed. He considers going by ship to Persia inde-
pendently and then making his way overland but is dissuaded. His
next entry has more significance than he realizes. It is little more
than three months until a war that will sweep across the world for
six years will break out in Europe and the time of waiting, and
opportunity for free movement, is now growing short.

Monday May 22, 1939

Today I went to Princeton and talked with Mr. James
B Cummings, on furlough from India. Then I had a
profitable talk with Dr. Zwemer.

Possibly to Horace the encounter with the great pioneer missionary to Muslims, Dr. Sam Zwemer, is the most significant
encounter of that day. Jim Cummings though is the man he needs
to meet. This is the day connections are made.

Jim Cummings is an MK, *a Mission kid*, born of renowned missionary parents in the North Punjab of India. He is serving in Gordon College, the Presbyterian college in Rawalpindi named after the founder of the Sialkot Mission. Jim's wife is also an MK. The Sialkot Mission works in an area of the Punjab up to the eastern edge of the Indus River and then crosses over into North Waziristan with a station at Kohat. It is unable to occupy Kohat for long periods because of shortage of personnel. North Waziristan lies between the Indus and the Afghan border.

Europe is ablaze with war. Grace is on a year's nursing course in New York City.

Monday October 2, 1939

I took up the studies at the National Bible Institute this fall and as far as the studies go I am enthusiastic. But I was faced with a real problem - funds exhausted and no source of income. I did not think it right to ask Dad for money - but I was in a fix. The problem had a wholesome effect - though at first I thought I must give up school again, which would make me ashamed. Grace and I prayed about it and finally had peace. Sunday the need was met by Johnny Roe, my staunch prayer supporter. Quite naturally the result was fresh enthusiasm.

Wednesday November 22, 1939

Grace and I, by mutual consent, broke our engagement. The decision was made tonight.

The last entry in Horace's five journals is dated Monday, December 11, 1939. He is fully certain that God's call to Him is to serve in Afghanistan and He will make it possible. He writes:

> *In prayer for Afghanistan I greatly eased the burden in making known my requests to God – in full confidence of faith knowing He waits to answer the prayers which He Himself inspired.*
>
> *Mr. Mallis, formerly of India has himself consented to arrange an appointment with me in January. This is a step in connection with my call to Afghanistan and I am grateful.*
>
> *I had a very fine talk with Dad concerning all these things. Dad is now confined to his bed after several heart attacks and when I am home we have fruitful fellowship together.*

Mac in India

1941 - Spring 1947

Mac has returned home to take care of his father who, since his three heart attacks, is bedridden. Mac stays by his father's bedside throughout his illness. When his father dies, Mac decides not to go to the funeral; he wants to remember Dad as he was.

In 1941 Horace, his two brothers and his mother and a friend drive across country to the West Coast. From San Francisco he boards a blacked-out Dutch freighter bound for India. His mother wonders whether she will ever see her middle son again. There are German sea raiders in the Pacific preying on Allied shipping.

It is all God's perfect timing for him. A few months later, at the end of the year, Japanese planes bomb Pearl Harbor in Hawaii and the Second World War is joined. From here on, passage to India for civilians is going to be severely limited.

Although the struggle is in Europe there is in the air a looming anticipation of war not far away even for the strong, secure and peaceful United States.

On the ship is a missionary doctor and his family, also heading for India. John Vroon, although not a Presbyterian, will be working at the Mission hospital in Taxila. They will be working for the same mission and will keep company as they travel across northern India to the annual meeting of the Sialkot Mission.

Some of what follows is conjecture. Mac arrives in Calcutta

(or possibly Bombay) in time to get across India by rail to Sialkot for the 1941 Mission meeting at the Christian Training Institute in October. As their ship steams into its berth, new impressions of a totally different world begin to accumulate. People, people, people! Where are the empty spaces? As soon as their luggage has been collected from the docks and cleared customs, the Vroons head off towards the rail station to acquire tickets across country to Sialkot through Delhi and Lahore while Mac sits atop the luggage on a flat bed bullock cart and follows them to the station at a more leisurely pace.

India is already at war. It is part of the British Empire. It is supplying troops to the Western Desert in North Africa and to the Persia and Iraq Force nearer home.

Mac's leading under God's clear direction is to work in Afghanistan. His goal is to eventually reach right into that closed country about which so little is really known. The Sialkot Mission, formed by the United Presbyterian Church of North America (UPCNA), is the only American mission that, pre-war, has work in the Northwest Frontier Province of India. Mac has met with the mission board representatives of the Sialkot Mission in Philadelphia in 1941. Agreement is reached for him to labor on the western fringes of the India mission area. During both of his terms he is an associate missionary of the Presbyterian mission and accepts the jurisdiction of the Board of Foreign Missions.

The Sialkot Mission has developed when communications between the home church and the field take months. Major decisions on the management of the Mission are wisely made on the field rather than by the very small head office back in Philadelphia.

Presbyterians have a great understanding of bureaucracy. They love it but somehow they love democracy more. They are hot on accountability. They manage to keep the bureaucrats they appoint under control so that the officers remain servants of the larger body that elects or appoints them rather than becoming masters or manipulators. This system of government of an organization can become a liability as well as a blessing for if it is to succeed it requires a constituency that is vocal, fair, well informed, varied and alert. It needs a middle ground larger than its fringes. In the days when there are up to one hundred missionaries of strong convictions brought together annually in Sialkot, it makes for strong interactions and is the high point of the missionary year.

The meeting takes place at the Christian Training Institute (CTI) in Sialkot each October. Missionaries returning from furlough gauge their timings to be back in time for Annual Meeting. It is the first point of touchdown for new missionaries. The institute, a boarding school, has a large campus with playing fields, running track and basketball courts and faces onto the broad expanse of the great open maidan (parade ground) on the north side of the city. The missionaries live rough. In the dormitories quickly fixed temporary curtains divide families from one another. The missahibas (single women missionaries) have another dormitory. The single men have another smaller room. In almost every mission there are many fewer single men and the married couples usually have imaginary pairings worked out for them. Mac is a fresh face for them to consider and from his arrival provides for them much speculation. Long-term missionary couples are inveterate matchmakers.

The Indian boys in the boarding school know that there will be a ten-day holiday for them in October not long after the Sialkot Convention.

After several days of devotions and worship there will be a week of business, often hotly debated. There will be present Indian observers from the Punjab Synod, the indigenous church arising from the mission's work, which is itself a Synod of the UPCNA.

They will be puzzled that such hotly expressed differing opinions during debates, especially about locations of missionaries but also about principles, practice and strategies, are matched by equally strong and apparently genuine affection once the matter has been voted upon. In Indian culture to differ from me so publicly and strongly means that you are my enemy. Mac will have been surprised that already the Mission is aware of the growing tide of the nationalist movement that will bring about independence for India. It needs to be looking towards its own strategy for an independent church that will be owning and managing property and disciplining itself.

His location during language study will have been decided at this meeting. Frequently new missionaries are not located for their language study where they will later be working. However, since Mac is an associate of the Sialkot Mission more attention will have been paid to his own expressed preferences. He is located in Campbellpur, just east of the Indus River, to live with *Uncle* Willie and *Aunt* Bertha Sutherland. One of the women missahibas on the same station, probably Eva Hewitt, is to have supervision of his language study. This is an excellent arrangement for two reasons. Campbellpur is close to the Northwest Frontier Province and living with a family follows the preferred arrangement for a new unmarried missionary. There is a lot of learning to do that is not at all related to language and a family with children in boarding school coming home for the winter is an excellent setting. *Uncle* Willie, who speaks with a thick Scots brogue, is not noted for the purity or fluency of his workmanlike Urdu. However, the saintly Eva will be an excellent guide not only to the language but also to things spiritual.

During that first winter season in India after Japan and USA become involved in the war the air is filled with rumors of military threat and dangers of air attack. India is soon to be facing a threat from the victorious Japanese armies approaching steadily and seemingly unstoppably from the east. The threat to India has always been perceived as through the Khyber Pass, never from the opposite direction.

Mac will need to learn Urdu first. This is a five-year course, which will include not only spoken fluency but also reading local newspapers written in script. His second preference would have been Pushto, the language of the Pukhtuns and the eastern Afghans but he does not appear to have been fluent in much more than the Pushto greetings. The pattern of four hours language study with an Indian teacher (munshi) paired with four hours private study each day memorizing is followed until it is time, as the hot season begins, to go to the hills for language school.

In April 1942 he goes for the first time up to Landour in the hills of North India for the Missionary Language School. In September or October he takes his First Year Language exams. Friendships made by new missionaries in language school will often endure through a lifetime and as among any group of young people with common interests romantic attachments are not unknown. After the exams are over he resumes back on the plains once more.

This pattern will be repeated for at least one further year before some relaxation to his timetable of language study, language study and more language study can be allowed.

What about this turbulent land of India to which he has come? Are there already signs of upheaval that will break the country apart when the war is over?

Almost a century earlier in 1857 the British are facing and dealing with a mutiny in the Indian Armed Forces. From this time onward there will be taking place a gradual absorption into the process of government qualified Indians, frequently British educated. These are the forerunners of the men who one day will govern India.

The British rule necessarily has to be by acquiescence of the people they rule. The ultimate military recourse that is available is British officered but largely indigenous. As a matter of practical wisdom, active military units are frequently limited to one particular faith. By and large it is a wise and relaxed rule by a judiciary and civil administration that becomes a byword for wisdom, fairness and integrity. It cannot survive, sitting atop a turbulent mass of diverse religious and feudal practices and expectations unless it is so.

Although many of the British administrators and judges are deeply committed Christians, their public practice is to seek to deal as fairly with Parsis, Buddhists, Sikhs, Hindus and Muslims as they do with Christians. In the days of William Carey at the beginning of the 19th century, Christian missionaries are excluded from British India and he himself works instead from a Danish settlement. The first licensing of Christian missionaries from overseas is secured in 1813.

At the end of 1885, the first meeting of the Indian National Congress takes place. This is the main instrument of the movement for independence and the party of majority government when it is attained.

The Muslims are uneasy. They would rather stay under British rule than be subject to the democratic majority of the would-be electorate that will surely vote on religious lines. The All India Muslim League is formed twenty years after the Congress. It seeks and receives from the British assurances of separate electorates and a *weightage* to compensate for their minority. They can breathe more easily but must remain politically alert and ready to sacrifice everything if necessary. Slowly however a new and radical idea is emerging. Muslims can never trust the Hindu majority to abide by guarantees of fair treatment to their own minority.

The idea espoused and articulated first by Sir Syed and then by the Punjabi poet Iqbal, of a part (or parts) of India run by Muslims for Muslims gains credence and favor and wholehearted opposition from Congress. In 1934 a brilliant and ascetic lawyer from Bombay, Mohammed Ali Jinnah, a disillusioned Congress member, becomes leader of the Muslim League and, eventually, architect of the drive for Pakistan.

The Muslims' right to their own land of Pakistan when the British leave India becomes the heart of the March 23, 1940 Resolution of the Muslim League in Lahore. From now on appeals for the continuing unity of British India fall on the deaf ears of almost a fifth of its population.

The whole of Mac's first term as a missionary is played out against the backdrop of these immense considerations of two mutually opposed nations struggling to emerge from a colonial administration like to neither of its successors. Famine occurs, riots and protests, strikes. Rumors of atrocities sweep across sections of the population and inflame them. Threats of invasion develop to almost the point of panic then diminish to nothing. The war ends and expectations of political rewards for cooperation rise. Several missions from London try to work out political ways forward. Wavell replaces Linlithgow as Viceroy and then he himself is replaced by Mountbatten. The end of British India is now near.

So also is Mac's first term. It has been a wonderful learning experience for him. The fascination of a multicultural polyglot India has captured his imagination and his heart. He counts this first term as nothing more than preparation time, an apprenticeship, a time for learning language, culture and custom and becoming acquainted with those with whom he will be working. He has had one particular stroke of immense good fortune. In 1946 Khan Zaman, the superlative servant, moves out to Campbellpur to work for Mac and from now on domestic arrangements are plain sailing and Mac is the envy of his contemporaries. When he comes back from his first furlough he will come back prepared for the work God has ahead for him.

He will return earlier than he expects.

A Spark Lights

Thanksgiving 1947 – December 1947

Thanksgiving is spent in Gujranwala with Norval's brother's family. After Dorothy is sufficiently recovered from her severe dysentery and vomiting, the team, in a small decrepit Army truck and a jeep, start out early in December towards India to locate the refugee columns moving towards Pakistan that they are to help.

Mac will go ahead in the jeep with Dick Wooten to arrange the dak (mail) bungalow where they can stay that night. Norval and Dorothy will follow later with Marie. When they get to Lahore they arrange a rendezvous over the border beyond Ferozepur. They will meet up there in the late afternoon. Mac admonishes the recent arrivals to the country, "Be sure to stay on the main road south from Lahore. Do not leave it for any reason whatsoever." He will be at the roadside waiting to guide them in.

When the light begins to fail there is still no sign of the rendezvous. Have they inadvertently gone past it? Has Mac intended some other road than the one they are on? Marie is sitting up in front beside the driver holding the gearshift in. The truck has no lights and crawls with the limited assistance of a hurricane lamp tied to the front bumper. The twilight flees before the darkness in only a few moments. The moon is almost full. Its silver light is throwing shadows of the roadside trees upon the road. On they drive.

Very limited communication with the other travelers, their escort or driver is possible. They have by now obviously come too far. They should go back and search the route they have already traveled. Norval is preparing to try to tell the driver this when ahead in the far distance a light flashes once, twice, thrice. The driver sighs his relief. Again ahead the lights of the jeep flash. Two very relieved men are waiting for them on the canal bank.

As they work, it is natural that Norval and Dorothy are together and Mac and Marie pair up. This is for Marie, with Mac alongside as interpreter, a unique introduction to the drama and scale of India, its problems, its tragedies, its courage and its patience and fortitude. People, people, people. It reminds Marie of the exodus of the Children of Israel as it might have been. Submerged in the bustle of a long line of refugees from horizon to horizon Mac breaks off from the vaccinations to explain or to translate. Already she is picking up a few words—ao, jao, bas, thik hai, kuchh nahin and kabardar! She is making notes of them and other words that she will ask about later.

With Indian Christians around, it only takes two to make a singing party and Mac is always ready to be one of them. Anything will serve to provide rhythm, fire-tongs or even a fork and a glass. The Psalms in their repeated Punjabi couplets get even these illiterate foreigners alongside them clapping the beat.

Mac is full of stories, Indian stories. Tales of his own experiences and of the experiences of missionaries of an earlier era. The Sialkot Mission is not yet a hundred years old but there are many stories, often miraculous stories. Stories of Kanaya and Ditt and other courageous illiterate new Christians who have come out of a Hindu outcaste background. Stories of Muslim converts to Christ, very few of them, who always seem motivated by some deeply personal supernatural experience of Christ. Stories of the cost that some of them have paid. Stories, too, of demonic possession and deliverance. Marie is not only catching understanding of his love for India and its people but also, strangely and unexpectedly, catching something of it herself.

Marie is observing not only Mac the man, but Mac the missionary. The two cannot be separated. He is living his faith out in both word and action. Uninhibited by language difficulty, he talks to strangers about God as easily and as readily as he talks about the dust and the wind and water to drink. Each day is dramatic with interest. Cameos lodge in her mind in all the confusion, of aged men carrying on their backs aged wives, of children leading blind companions, of the stupid almost laughable pieces of irrelevant clutter that people are carrying, of kindnesses innumerable among people who have lost almost everything except their humanity. Stirring in her mind is an appreciation of the immense strength of the religious idea of Islam that can drive people to suffer so patiently and silently for a distant hope. She knows that similar events are taking place in the other direction also.

After the columns have halted for the night—it is turning cold and very few of the refugees have adequate bed covering—the team wearily turns back home. Mrs. Hogg once again produces one of her superlative meals from the supplies she has brought from Lahore or found in the local market or bazar. Mac then helps them to relax.

Mac loves to sing. Back home in New Jersey, he and his two brothers often sang in church or at home as a trio. Now he will either get his team singing carols with him or he sings unaccompanied as they travel. He seems to know all the hymns by heart and many spirituals and popular songs also.

Marie is enjoying his light-heartedness amongst the surrounding tragedy and finding herself looking forward to the end of each day. There is usually time for a walk together before or after dinner if they aren't singing. The night sky is so clear, the

stars so bright and so many, the noises strange and diminishing
in volume as sleep settles over the flat, flat land and the twinkling
of a thousand fires give way to darkness. There is so much to talk
about—God, their faith, their families, their past and their separate plans for the future. Both are recognizing they share many
interests and ideals.

Mac, she is concluding after only a week on the road, is one
of those rare *extra special* people with a quality of inner radiance
that it becomes a privilege to know. How fortunate to have this
remarkable man as their team leader.

She is finding herself completely happy in these strange almost
desert surroundings and rarely homesick for the Swedish Christmas festivities of North Park and Selah. She is recognizing, initially with astonished surprise, that her happiness is increasingly
responsive to her proximity to Mac. She is aware too that Mac is
enjoying her company and is as ready and willing to ask questions
of her as to respond to her own. She has found his arm around her
cushioning her against bumps on a couple of occasions when she
falls asleep against him in the back seat of the truck.

She wonders whether Norval and Dorothy are noticing anything, she is trying to disguise the unexpected emotions that are
stirring her. Neither she nor Mac realize that by the time they
reach Amsterdam on the way out the Christys have decided the
couple are busy falling in love and are trying to give them all the
space they need.

Marie's Diary

December 3 – December 14

Only a short diary of Marie's is available about her experiences. It is brief and many questions are unanswered.

December 3, 1947

We three Babes in the Woods leave Gujranwala with an Indian driver who speaks no English. We speak no Punjabi. He stops in the bazar, takes his tommy gun and stalks off to reappear twenty minutes later.

We stop several times along the road for him to smoke his pipe. When we reach Lahore he can't find the CMS House. Finally we arrive, have tea and check over 'stores.' I search for coffee and coffeepot.

Camels are snooty, no matter how moth-eaten.

We meet Dr. Holland, son of Sir Henry Holland of eye surgery fame.

Spend the night at Forman Christian College, Lahore with Ross Wilsons.

Am a bit squeamish when I see some large Muslim with a wicked looking gun.

December 4, 1947

The lorry calls for me an hour late. Am a bit startled to climb into a truck and find myself facing five armed Punjabi soldiers. Pretended it was an everyday affair.

Had breakfast in Lahore with British at CMS House. Finally had everything loaded and ready to go. Were warned not to let drive because he knocked over anything in the way.

We careened off down the road dodging between tongas, bicycles, pedestrians, dogs, buffaloes and whatnot much in the fashion of a skier dodging between trees. The dust – a fine sandy sort of dust – covered us from head to foot and kept the visibility down to nothing.

We got lost in every village.

Finally wound up in a Presbyterian hospital camp where we had our picnic lunch on the verandah while the staff gathered round to pass the time of day.

It was amusing the way we were helped along by Muslims, Hindus, Sikhs who a few weeks ago were cutting each other's throats.

Crossing the border was an experience! The gate was closed and heavily guarded. We were checked across very carefully.

As it began to get dark we were sure we had lost our way but just as we were about to give up we saw a light flash on.

Sure enough it was our Dak bungalow and there were Mac and Mr. Wooten waiting for us.

After a great struggle we had a supper of beans and scrambled eggs – and so to bed.

December 5, 1947

We spent this morning going through our supplies and taking inventory. Mac and I went into the bazaar, which was closed, but we were offered tea by an opium-smoking shopkeeper. The flies were thick but I downed my tea.

The Sikhs with their black beards, flashing eyes and long curved swords fascinate me. Glad I don't have to be out after dark.

Mac had a wonderful opportunity to speak with the magistrate about God.

On our way out an old Christian gave us three eggs. He was simply glad we had come. Mac paid him.

In the afternoon we went to work. Such a pitiful chaos! We gave out sulfa, paludrine, aspirin and vaccinated every child in sight. Saw a number of cases of drippy smallpox. Took pictures riding camels.

Came home to a bucket of hot water. What luxury!

Mac sang all the way home. In fact he is always singing. What a marvelous disposition. Sang Christmas carols after dinner.

Saturday December 6, 1947

We started out early to vaccinate as many as possible of our column. At first armed soldiers of the 8th Punjab Regiment were with us.

It must have been a riot to see us dashing along the road jumping up on oxcarts and pulling people down off camels to be vaccinated. I think they could tell from the gleam in our eyes that we were going to do something or other to them.

In my great zeal I kept forgetting to look where I was going and was forever finding myself in the embrace of ox horns.

We had a squad of soldiers to help us too. We sort of relieved each other for tea and so on.

In the afternoon we ran the usual dispensary.

Quit early to go home and move camp. After dinner we loaded up the two trucks and started off in the bright starlight. As usual Mac sang for us. We never tire of his singing either. I also discovered he has a nice shoulder.

Falling in Love

Sunday December 7, 1947

Mac took the Indian Christians to the village church. I stayed home to help Mrs. Hogg get the 'house' settled. Also started lunch.

In the afternoon we went out and set up dispensary. In the evening we just sat around after dinner. Mac told stories of Indian magic and spirits with the bowl of pickles as a background.

Monday December 8, 1947

Set up our dispensary early in the morning. Came home about five. I was so happy to see how clean and healthy some of the wounds looked which we had dressed before! It is worthwhile after all.

There was trouble about our rooms and the men finally had to move.

Mac and I went walking before dinner.

Tuesday December 9, 1947

I stayed home to watch the stuff today so that Mrs. Hogg

could go out to the column. It has been a most pleasant day. Of course I've had Hindus and Sikhs peeking in the windows and I don't dare leave the place unguarded but it's been fun anyway.

In mid-afternoon I heard a terrible row going on. Next thing I knew the sweeper had taken a club to the chaprasi (messenger) and the chaprasi had taken an axe (our axe) to the sweeper. Our two cooks, John and Inayat, barged in to stop the argument. I was afraid there was going to be a murder right before my eyes.

Just after I had taken the pins out of my hair, who should arrive but Colonel Babar. Colonels are the same in every army. He is very solicitous of our welfare – wants to bring us fruit and white bread – also wants us to stay at where he himself is headquartered.

Informed me he has no wife. As I said before, colonels, or officers generally for that matter, are the same in every army.

Dorothy says he asked them to tell me not to stay home again. He was lost.

I was so glad when Mac drove in! If I were just out here for adventure I might make something of this colonel business – but as it is – no.

Wednesday December 10, 1947

We packed up this am and moved from Abohar to Fazilka.

As soon as we were settled we went to the market. Immediately we were surrounded by scores of Hindus and Sikhs. We were evidently the first Europeans they had seen in a long time.

We hadn't been there fifteen minutes when who should appear but the colonel. He certainly keeps track of us.
Later in the afternoon Mac and I went to the Indian padri's house and through the bazar.
The refugee train came about five p.m. Mac and I went through part of it and found much smallpox. Did a little vaccinating.
The colonel sent the coffee he had promised, too!
After dinner Mac made coffee and built a fire in the fireplace. We had a beautiful evening singing spirituals and watching the embers die. Mac is extra special.

Thursday December 11, 1947

We got up at the crack of dawn to rush out to the camp to vaccinate. When we got there, before seven am, the camp was bare. They had all gone, so Mac and I strolled through the town before breakfast.
As usual the colonel came to pay his morning call. We had coffee.
A little later we had tea at the home of the Indian padri.
In the afternoon Mac and I went for a long walk in the country.
About 4:30 the train came in and with that gleam in our eyes we went out to vaccinate. We had a very successful two hours.
After dinner we went to the meeting of Indian Christians. Mac led the service. It was a real pleasure – and a beautiful evening.

Friday December 12, 1947

Had a late breakfast, talked a while and were sort of lazy.
Mac, Mrs. Hogg and I went to the bazar. Had fun.
After lunch we packed and started off from Fazilka to
Abohar where we picked up supplies including some bundles
of clothes which along with Mac's arm and shoulder made
a most comfortable and pleasant trip.
Arrived at the rest house at Mauhnona about five p.m.
This was our starting point for the last trek and our first
home on the road. It is a quiet peaceful place away from
any village with all its noises.
Hope we stay here a few days. We are sort of expecting
Dick Wooten's party to join us here any time.
The days are so very beautiful. It can't possibly be almost
Christmas. If I weren't so happy here I would be lonesome
for all the Christmas music, lutefisk and fun at school and
North Park church. As it is I wouldn't trade, not even for
Winston's music, and that's saying a lot.

Saturday December 13, 1947

We worked a little today but the column is small, only
about 3,000 people.
After dinner Mac and I went for a long walk down the
road towards Dubwali. When we came home we made
coffee and sat around and talked until the unheard of hour
of 11:15.
After all that coffee I couldn't sleep.

Sunday December 14, 1947

We attended service along with the British unit at the Indian padri's home. The service was held in the courtyard with the men sitting on a canvas and us on rope beds. There was a horse, and a buffalo calf, right with us. Jalal played the harmonium. I couldn't help but think of the stained glass windows and the organ at North Park.

From there we went to work. I was sent out to sit in the sunshine because of my cold. Of course I was joined by His Nibs, the Colonel. That charming gentleman doesn't waste any time. And I think it's time for me to be careful.

We stopped work at four to have tea with Wooten's party. All the Indians including the padri and his daughter sat on the floor. After tea there was much singing.

As we were driving home we saw a sliver of new moon with a planet which Mac thought was Venus, directly above it. The whole thing was above a pink afterglow of the sunset. I have never seen a lovelier sky. It could have been the Star of Bethlehem. Just before leaving I saw a string of camels against the horizon. Mac sang all the way home and I was completely happy even though I couldn't breathe with my cold.

Christmas at Rawalpindi

Two people who have met for the first time only a month ago in America are in the north of Pakistan. Although as yet they hardly realize it they are falling or already have fallen in love. Time is running out also, the purpose that brought them together. Medical help to the refugee columns is coming to an end as the stragglers come in.

For Marie her journey to Pakistan is an interlude of short duration in a larger plan of things for her life. Although the door to China is closing she is not yet seeing India or Pakistan as an alternative. In six months she expects to be back home at North Park, Chicago, completing her course in Missions. God will surely direct her from that point on. The Swedish Covenant Church has work in other countries if China should close and that closure is by no means certain.

Mac is not a confirmed bachelor, he would welcome a helpmeet, yet he knows it is unlikely that he will find a wife who will share with him his enthusiasm for service in a hard-core Muslim country inhabited by Pathans or Afghans. That is God's call for his life; he has no doubt. Whoever he marries will need to share that enthusiasm and also his love for those people.

yes — ours for the Pakistani

Mac asks whether for Christmas Marie would like to come up with him beyond Rawalpindi to his old Mission station at Campbellpur as well as to Taxila where he is to be located as chaplain when his furlough is over. Norval and Dorothy will be spending Christmas in Gujranwala but it wouldn't be difficult to go on the further 150 miles by road or train. Perhaps they might even get use of the jeep.

This is a welcome invitation.

By Christmas the team has dropped off Mrs. Hogg in Lahore and has returned to Gujranwala in Pakistan. Marj and Wilbur's children are home from boarding school in Landour in India. Marj has gone over to collect them and they have not had too much trouble on the journey home across the border. They are delighted to welcome Uncle Norval and to become acquainted with their new Aunt Dorothy.

At 9 a.m. on Christmas Eve the travelers to Taxila start out with a bedroll on the bumper of the jeep, two suitcases on the hood, two men and various bundles in the front seat, two bedrolls, three large suitcases and a gallon thermos jug of water, two jerricans of gasoline and Mac and Marie in the back. They pick up the Grand Trunk Road and head north. The first of the winter rains has come, the earth shoulders to the narrow double carriageway are badly rutted and drivers both ways stick to the hard surface until the head on collision seems inevitable. There are many examples along the way that avoiding action has been attempted too late.

Marie has not long before read Kipling's *Kim*, recommended to her as the best introduction to India. She knows of the great Grand Trunk Road that runs across northern India from Calcutta to the Khyber Pass. This is new country to her and very different terrain. At Kharian they climb up onto the lower hills of the

Potwar plateau and then come down towards the most westerly of the Punjab rivers, the Jhelum.

Just to the south Alexander the Great has, more than two millennia ago, won a wonderful victory against Porus in his first battle against elephant mounted troops. Mac knows the story and enjoys telling it to the woman beside him.

In Alexander's day the river was known as the Hydaspes. After marching across Persia and Afghanistan he crossed the Indus at Ohind just north of Attock. He had come on down from Taxila where King Ambhi offered to provide him with elephants to fight his own rival, Porus. The battle itself took place in midsummer of 326 BC. The snowmelt would have swollen the river and early rains of the summer monsoon made it even more difficult. Porus had more than twice as many infantry, three hundred chariots and a hundred elephants. Crossing over the river upstream at night with his crack troops and his own cavalry, Alexander won his last great victory and made the vanquished king of the Chhach doab, the land lying between the Jhelum and Chenab Rivers, his friend and ally.

The city at the river crossing teems with men far different than the Punjabis Marie has previously encountered. Often their turbans, and their baggy shirts and trousers are black. They are frequently tall, wear large mustachios, look like brigands, carry rifles almost to a man and wear bandoliers of bullets and brightly colored waistcoats. They walk with long strides and with deference to no one. They look you straight in the eye. Their shoes are thick leather strap sandals soled with, it appears, pieces of tire rubber. They speak gutturally, their language sounding somewhat similar to the German prisoners of war she has encountered a different world months ago.

There, in Jhelum City, they have morning tea with a diminutive missionary nurse who is busy with her own Christmas decorations at the Good Samaritan Hospital. Evva explains the town is full of Pathans fighting their way along the course of the Jhelum River towards the heart of Kashmir. They aren't doing very well; they have expected to be back home by the end of the year. No one has molested her or interfered in her work with women and children.

Further towards Rawalpindi, Mac points out the stone ruins where tradition says Alexander has buried his horse Bucephalus. This is a hilly country, wilder and less fertile than the plains of the alluvial Punjab.

To the right as they drive is a distant line of snow covered peaks, the Pir Panjal that skirt Kashmir. The nearer hills are almost all in the hands of Pakistan's irregulars.

Rawalpindi, with the Margalla / Murree hills in close proximity, has an immediately different feel to Lahore, Gujranwala and the Punjab towns in India.

Mac explains, as they shop for a few Christmas gifts at Esajees, that most of these men she is seeing are not usual Pindi residents but part of the huge influx of warriors, Mahsuds and Wazirs, Khattaks and Afridis, that have come from across the Indus to save Kashmir for Pakistan. They are natural born fighters. Children grow up in tribal territory with a rifle as a plaything. A different law prevails. The British have not been able to subdue them. Had they not stopped to loot at Baramula, the capital city of Srinagar would already have fallen to them. It is pretty well stalemate in Kashmir now.

It is interesting to observe the change in Mac, smelling the scent of home, meeting and greeting people in the streets and shops that know him, throwing happy guttural greetings to the Pathans he has never met before. They respond warmly to a kindred spirit.

In Pindi Mac takes Marie to the Davis' for lunch. Carl will

later work alongside them in Lyallpur while Agnes, refreshingly Covenant in background, still has among her treasures from home a pound of the Swedish addiction, Hill's coffee. It has never tasted better.

Now it is a mere twenty odd miles further on to Taxila. They drive on past Nicholson's monument, through the pass and down to Serai Kala. Almost home! Mac is welcomed at the hospital bungalows like a lost son by a long mustachio'd Pakistani hill man. He comes running, drying his hands as he runs, from Miss McConnell's kitchen. He is followed by his sons and daughters and hobbling behind them all comes his wife, Mir Jan. After the hugs and salaams and a few urgent questions Mac manages to introduce Marie to Khan Zaman. Among the bright-eyed children is his oldest daughter, Zebunnissa. These are some for whom Mac has been buying gifts and he conscripts Marie to help suitably package them for the morrow.

Marie writes in her diary:

> *Reached Taxila about 6 p.m. Christmas Eve. Attended a drama, had a late dinner and went to bed. I was more than thrilled with all the beautiful hills. It was like being home.*

Thursday December 25, 1947

> *We opened our packages at Karsgaard's after breakfast.*
> *After church Mac and I went for a walk.*
> *Lunch was an Indian meal with the Christian staff and their families out on the lawn. The pilau was too hot for me.*
> *After tea Mac and I walked again.*
> *Dinner was at Karsgaard's. Roast goose.*

Afterwards Mac and I walked in the beautiful moonlight.
Just after we got to bed some carol singers came around.
They sang until almost four am.
It was a beautiful Christmas but I missed our traditional
festivities.

Friday December 26, 1947

Mac and I drove Karsgaard's car to Campbellpur. Had
lunch with Sutherlands. It was a beautiful day and Mac
was especially nice. It was a ride I won't soon forget.

I think this is Marie's private shorthand in her diary for a secret
she wishes to keep for a while though it is going to become more
and more difficult. I conjecture something like this happened.

About eight miles beyond Taxila, across the great Wah plain,
a line of limestone hills rise. The hills are quarried for cement and
stone. The Dhamra River flows to the east of the hills and the
Haro to the west, both eventually feeding into the Indus. Between
the two rivers, in a valley where the Grand Trunk Road threads
its way, a multitude of refreshing springs sparkle loose. It is said
that the Moghal Emperor Akbar, observing these springs where
his caravan to Kashmir rested one hot summer exclaimed "Wah,
wah!" (Our equivalent would probably be a long 'Wooooow!') That
gave the village, about a mile from the present road, its name.
The old village of Wah, with a Moghal Pavilion, a walled
bathing pool and large Moghal period gardens and orchards with
watercourses fed by the springs and by the waters of the Dhamra,
belongs to the Hayat Khan family. The male villagers still follow the custom of stopping in their tracks and turning their faces
to the wall away from any woman of family status they might

chance encounter within the village. It is the most delectable spot between Taxila and Campbellpur.

As the Karsgaard car comes down the slope towards the narrow stone arched bridge across the Dhamra, Mac turns left off from the main road towards the Wah gardens. He has often stopped here for a rest when making the long cycle or motorcycle ride to Taxila from Campbellpur. It is a favorite spot. Mac is acquainted with members of the Wah family. He shows Marie the Mahal and bathing pool before walking with her through the gardens. Large goldfish abound in the watercourses and hover almost motionless in spots shaded by the overhanging mango and loquat branches.

They sit on a vantage seat and watch the fish for a while, saying nothing, savoring the moment and their own private proximity.

Mac takes from his pocket a packet wrapped in gift paper with the clumsy effect only men can achieve. "I want you to have this," he says.

Marie opens it slowly. It is a copy of the Revised Standard Version of the New Testament. It has been first published only the previous year and it has been one of Mac's first purchases on his return home on furlough.

She turns to the flyleaf. It is inscribed—*To my dear Marie, Christmas, 1947 H.J. McGuill.*

She says nothing for a moment or so and it is Mac who breaks the silence. He tells her, simply, that he loves her and that he dares to hope, after they have known each other longer, that she will reciprocate his affection. He has wanted to write—*To my dearest Marie, Christmas 1947, Mac*—but that would have been premature. She is now seeing the land where he lived and will continue to live. He hopes that by the time their assignment finishes she will be sure of herself and she will know whether this will be where she will be willing to spend the rest of her life. Meanwhile he will not press her for a response and his love for her will remain a secret between them. It will make their working situation easier and will avoid possible problems.

He looks at her; his eyes are shining. He waits.

She reaches over and takes his hand in hers and presses it. She says simply "Thank you, Mac, I'll pray about it" and clasps his gift to her heart. The light in her eyes is the only other response.

Marie's diary continues:

> *In the afternoon we attended a tea given by the Hennesseys for the cement factory workers.*
> *Left for Pindi in time to have dinner at Davis.' Some of the Friends were there too.*
> *Mac took a terrific ribbing about stargazing. (We did some too)*

The following day they leave immediately after breakfast for Lahore, picking up Norval and Dorothy at Gujranwala on the way.

Marie and Mac

Marie and Mac marry in August 1948 in Hawthorne, New Jersey. He is completing his interrupted furlough. Mac is one week younger than Marie.

> *July 30 1949*
> *Dear Freda,*
> *I am sitting here in my underwear because I can't stand*
> *any more clothes on. We went to the shore to spend a night*
> *and a day with Mac's brother and even tho' I was very*

careful I am burned to a crisp. Mac is too. All the time I wasn't in the water I was in the shade or covered up but nevertheless I am burned. Oh misery!

We had a great surprise which distressed us not a little. On Wednesday we were notified by the Mission Board that they had a sailing for us on August 22 - just three weeks from Monday! I don't see how we can possibly make it but I suppose we will have to. We still have quite a bit of shopping to do and all the packing. Besides that we have to go to a conference near Pittsburgh on Monday and stay there until Thursday, that is August 1 through 4.

We are going to take the train because it is about a ten-hour drive and by taking a night train we can spend Monday doing many things in New York and then catch the train and be in Pittsburgh in the morning. We will do the same coming back. As I may have mentioned, life with the McGuills is never dull - may it never be.

The weather here is simply awful. The humidity has been up in the eighties and the temperature in the nineties so you have an idea how we feel. Both of us have had prickly heat because we are never dry. Can't even get dry after a bath to put one's clothes on. We have been able to sleep nights though which is a blessing. How has it been at home? I know if it is hot at least the nights are cool and it isn't so humid. I had a nice birthday. That was the day we drove to the shore.

You might tell the girls that I have gone so far as to get at a list for the layette and will be buying it just as soon as we get back from the conference.

Marie

Aboard SS Flying Cloud - August 29, 1949

Dear Freda,

We didn't think we would ever make it, but somehow we did—after leaving several articles behind and several errands pushed off on others. What a feeling of relief we had when we actually clambered on board and saw our luggage-strewn cabin. A number of people from Mac's church and his family were there to see us off. However they couldn't stay until the ship sailed. We had to be on board by four o'clock in the afternoon but the ship didn't actually sail until 9:20 at night.

Because we were so exhausted we did not stay up for the departure but went to bed right after supper. When it was apparent we were under way we made an effort and managed to sit up in bed and gaze for a few minutes through the porthole – that was all that we conceded to the occasion. We recognized the lights of the Empire State Building and 'The Light that never Fails' on the Metropolitan building and then went back to sleep.

Our cabin is on the port side just off the deck, it is rather spacious and comfortable. Our fellow passengers are friendly and interesting; a vice-consul and his wife (whom we had known slightly in Lahore) on their way to take up new duties in Karachi; a young lady also in consular service; three Indian students returning from their studies in America; and another missionary from our Mission.

The food is fairly good. Meals are a little on the heavy side meant for men who work on the ship, but they are quite tasty. We have decided the cook must be Creole or Latin American, judging from his very interesting and spicy meat sauces. The Ship's officers eat in the same dining room but at different tables so we don't get to know them very well.

Until about the third day out the seas were as calm and beautiful as one could wish but then we ran into the tail end of a hurricane. The ship lurched and tossed and rolled in the manner approved in all sea stories; the sea was rough enough to satisfy the most hardy. No one got seasick possibly because the rough part began at night when the more vulnerable passengers were in their bunks. But everything moveable in the cabins shifted around. Drawers yawned, suitcases sprawled, chairs slid and our basket of fruit upset its contents over the floor. Doors banged and the ship groaned and creaked in every joint. We didn't sleep. We lay on our tummies gripping the edges of the bunks, trying to identify by every thud or crash the more mobile parts of our equipment. The captain decided that if the ship were going to stay in one piece we had better turn round which we did ' in the teeth of the booming gale.' When we were turning we came broadside to the waves and the rocking we got then was terrific. By that time our cabin floor was littered with oranges, peaches, lemons, a jar of marmalade which slid loose and tobogganed from our dresser top (smashed, of course) Mac's razor and various other things. In trying to replace some of the things Mac opened the medicine chest on the wrong pitch of the ship and a bottle of shaving lotion slid out and shattered in the washbasin. All this time Mac was admonishing me "Don't get excited," which grieved me because I wasn't excited. This vigorous existence continued most of the next day with the ship now heading back to New York at a greatly reduced speed.

Finally, about three o'clock in the afternoon the sea became calm enough so that the ship could be turned and we resumed our voyage toward Pakistan. Since then all has been calm.

We should be in Karachi about September 17 or 19. Then after a trip upcountry we should be in Taxila by the end of the following week.   Marie

by train

August 29th (continued)

Now with some leisure from packing and hustling we can attend to the more vital inner preparation for the time ahead. We feel inadequate; we know we are inadequate but we have laid hold for help on One who is mighty. Having been in Pakistan before, we do not underestimate the difficulties of Muslim work. But neither do we measure the task with any inward misgivings. Joshua 1:9 was a staunch weapon that was placed in our hands in the service at Grace Church (Mac's brother's church) before we left. We have other promises too as weapons in our armory which are mighty through God to the overthrowing of strongholds. We had one such in our reading this morning, "They that sow in tears shall reap in joy. He that goeth forth with weeping, bearing precious seed, shall come again with rejoicing, bringing his sheaves with him." We feel strengthened by these for the work ahead. Our opportunities are tremendous and we know that the Lord intends to reap a harvest in Pakistan. He will honor His Word, glorify His Son, and reward a hundred-fold all of His people there at home who so faithfully enable us to be out here for Him.

(Up to this point this letter has been the original of some carbon copies which we are sending to a number of friends. But from here on it is for you, Freda)

We thank you a thousand times for the money, Freda. We do appreciate more than you will ever know all the things you have done for us. But we didn't use it for a layette as you suggested because we had already purchased all that we would need with the other $25 and some money from the outfit money Mac's church gave us.

We did use part of it for records. You know we both enjoy music so much and we didn't feel we should spend church money on what might be considered a luxury. We bought six long-playing records which will give us several hours of music. We plan to have music with our dinner at night. We went very carefully over the catalogue of recordings and picked out a good variety. We have two symphonies, one record of organ music of Bach, one record of almost classical sacred selections sung by Helen Traubel, one record of Negro spirituals, one of Mac's favorite recordings of Grieg. Seems we have something else too but I can't remember what it is now. The portable player we got was quite inexpensive and plays regular records as well as the new long-playing ones. We are only taking out the long playing because they are unbreakable and have so much more music per record, about thirty to forty-five minutes. We will think of you every time we enjoy the music which will be almost every day.

My mother's needs are very few and so there will probably be some of that money from her inheritance left for a funeral. If there isn't I still have enough bonds to cover it. I cashed enough bonds to buy some furniture for our house in Pakistan but the rest I left for an emergency. It is certain that we will never have any money laid aside for an emergency and we both felt that instead of spending that money for things we could no doubt use in Pakistan it *would be best to leave it. It isn't much, about $400 when the bonds mature.*

At this moment Mac is playing chess with one of the Indian boys. I too have been having lessons in that favorite game of his.

Thursday we are passing Gibraltar. Our only stop will be Alexandria where I hope to see Kirkie.

Love,

Mac & Marie

(Marie's mother died three years later in Montana August 1952)

At Work in Taxila

American Mission Hospital, Taxila, West Pakistan

February 26, 1950

Dear Freda,

How goes the battle? Hope it is warming up a little for you. For the first time since November I am warm through and through. It feels wonderful. This is like a nice May day at home. Our living room is up to 60 today. In a couple of weeks it will be really warm.

Mac is away in Lahore - 200 miles - to hear one of the world's greatest living theologians, Emil Brunner, who is making an extensive lecture tour. I believe he is from Holland or Germany or maybe Switzerland. He has written many books and is much discussed in seminaries all over the world. Mac has also gone to get literature for the hospital to distribute during the busy season which is just beginning and will be in full swing by the middle of March.

We have two new buildings which will be ready to use soon. One is a women's ward and the other a chapel. The chapel will be used for several things besides services and will be a most useful building. As soon as that is open we will have another much needed room in our house. What should be our living room is now our chapel.

We have just had a conference of the missionaries working on what is called the North-West Frontier and nearby in the Punjab. The conference was on our compound with about thirty missionaries present. The thing that thrilled me was that nearly all were young people. There were two or three in their third term, two or three or four in their second term, one older couple in their last term and all the others were first termers. The meetings were certainly inspirational and informative. Some of the people were from Ireland, some from Scotland, some from England, some from New Zealand and some from America. They represent several different missions varying from the Church of England to a Holiness group.

A change has been suggested to our location by the executive committee of the mission. It has to be ratified by the location committee and I believe voted on by the members of the mission. It is that we go to Kohat where we went for the Christmas service. That city is right on the edge of the tribal territory about which I wrote after our visit there. It is a very nice city with many trees and beautiful gardens because they have irrigation. We would both like to go there but we would hate to leave the great opportunities which are here too. Anyway the decision is not in our hands.

We would be taking over the contacts and following in the footsteps of Miss Flora Davidson who wrote 'Hidden Highways,' a book you should read. She is now in her seventies and for the past very few years she has not been

*living in Kohat because she hasn't been able to live alone.
We would rent a large house and share it with her. I think
we would have two separate arrangements for cooking etc,
sort of divide the house like a duplex. Kohat is a place that
has been prayed about for years that a missionary couple
would take over.*

*I must stop and get on with my work, am still hard at
the language. About the first of May I will be leaving my
hearth and home and going up to the hills to school. Mac
will be staying down here until the middle of July and then
will take his six weeks up with me, the language exams
will be in September, at least the orals will. Probably the
writtens will be in October. Then I can let up from six
hours a day to two, which will be a blessing.*

Marie

(The Kohat and Kurram areas had been under the agreed
jurisdiction of the Church Missionary Society (CMS) of England
but they had turned it over to the Sialkot Mission in 1921 since
they were themselves unable to man it. Flora Davidson was a
redoubtable Englishwoman who had been invited by the Sialkot
Mission to "enter Kohat and share in the work there" and in 1925
she had done so. For much of the time she had been alone in this
Pathan tribal town. During her residence there had been much
tribal unrest and fighting with British and Indian troops.)

Mac and Marie are the first representatives to be appointed
by the Sialkot Mission to Kohat but they eventually are unable to
take up the appointment.

Mac Writes Home

Taxila, November 10, 1952

Dear Friends,

One day a few weeks ago when Sunday School was over, the people came out the door of the church and stood around greeting one another and talking among themselves as they always do, just as they do at home. The children rushed out to play. The women, dressed in their colorful Punjabi clothes, stood in a group by themselves chatting away for dear life. The men were standing in several small groups on the church lawn.

The Men's Class had been well attended that day, but among them all I noticed a stranger and asked someone who he was. I was wrongly informed that he was a visiting relative of one of our members, so was about to pass on with simply a greeting to him

Marie, never one to miss an opportunity, pulled my sleeve and told me that the young man should be spoken to. I drew him aside and asked him a few questions. He was a very troubled young man, and not a Christian. He had come to the Christians' Sunday School in order to learn something of the religion, as he expressed it, where there is love and sympathy and kindness. He knew no more about it than that. He felt nothing greater than a need for love and kindness, and with this vague, wistful longing he had come to our class. It was a joy to point him to the One who can fully satisfy his longings, the Lord Jesus Christ, who can also save him from his sins. The young man continues under our instruction.

It reminds us of a verse in Titus, "But when the kindness of God our Savior, and His love toward man, appeared . . . He saved us."

I have just now come home from preaching to the outpatients at the hospital, and Marie has gone with other Christian women to witness in the non-Christian homes in Taxila village. The blessings of a stable government under peaceful conditions continue to prevail in this country. Some few are roused to opposition from time to time, but on the whole people are friendly and courteous. They listen to our message, read our tracts and booklets and every now and then the Lord leads us to individuals who are really hungry-hearted (I have 15 or 20 such on my prayer list just now).

We know that many would like to accept the message of salvation but are held back by fear of ostracism, boycott, or worse, because the courtesy and the hearing granted to the missionary is never granted to the convert, as you know. Missionaries are safe; inquirers are threatened; converts are often in danger. For this reason we have to observe one who professes belief for a fairly long period of time – after the first enthusiasm passes we have to look to see if he is rooted in a vital faith. If not, he can never stand the withering blast that is sure to come to him.

One man in particular shows real promise of vital faith right now. He has had a New Testament and teaching from us, and more detailed instruction from another missionary of our group. He professed his faith to us, and I asked him to return to his non-Christian village (in a very hard area) to continue his study and his profession there. Every report we hear is good, and we thank the Lord that he continues in the faith, makes his witness known to all, and travels for miles in difficult mountain country in order to fellowship with other believers. May God grant him true, unfeigned faith, and the grace to hold fast his boldness and the glorying of his hope firm unto the end, as it says in the epistle to the Hebrews.

One such witness in that mountain area can be a powerful factor in winning others. In fact two others from that very village appear to be very near, themselves, to an understanding and a reception of the Gospel. The cold season is coming on and patients are fewer in the hospital just now.

Chrysanthemum buds are beginning to open in the garden, and the tall clumps of poinsettias blaze with their scarlet fire. The ground is very dry, and powdery with thick dust; we are very much in need of rain.

Spiritually we need the refreshing rain of revival blessings too. The Devil is hard at work in more ways than one, trying to engender strife, split up groups and divide congregations. That we wrestle not against flesh and blood is a fact that we must learn very early in our experience. But thank the Lord, Satan is a defeated foe and our Lord Jesus Christ has gained the victory. May all God's people live in His triumph!

Sincerely yours, in His fellowship,
Mac

The British wives have observed curiously what Marie has been doing while Mac is engaged with the Pakistani Christian men. No staying at home for her! Many of the families are sweeper fami-

lies and while the men are working, Marie, clad in shalwarqamiz, has her women's Bible Study groups. Because most of the women cannot read, she teaches them. They gather in their various basti (slum) groups as soon as she arrives and sit down on the brick paving in front of their homes wherever is better, sun or shadow.

She wears from her neck the literacy posters showing alif, be, pe and patiently drills her women and girls, pointing with a stick until they can make the right sounds for the right symbols. When she is through she admonishes them to show their husbands what they have written on their slates and to teach their husbands also. Now it is time for Marie to look at the various sick babies that are brought to her and to listen to the women share their medical and family concerns.

Mac Moves On Alone

Taxila, West Pakistan

May 10, 1953

Dear Frances and all the family,

Mac passed away yesterday after a week's illness with polio.

How little we know from one day to the next what is going to happen.

He woke up with a severe headache a week ago yesterday morning. By evening he had a fever of 101. Sunday he had a fever but was able to walk to his bed. Here when one has fever we always think of malaria first.

Monday morning when I was going to help him out of bed his legs wouldn't work. We didn't think it was polio at first because he didn't follow the usual pattern. The leg paralysis was a terrible shock, but we felt we could overcome that if it remained.

Tuesday afternoon he told me that his breathing was becoming increasingly difficult. We got oxygen from the nearby cement company.

By Wednesday morning it was apparent we had to get him

*in an iron lung. The military hospital in Pindi had one so
we rushed him there. He was better for two days and then
began to slip.*

*He couldn't sleep either day or night and I think lack of
sleep just wore him out. By the time he went he was pretty
generally paralyzed but was still able to squeeze my hand
with both of his just a little.*

*Had he lived some or most of the paralysis might have left
him, but one never knows. He was wonderful through it
all, he never complained and had a heavenly expression on
his face all the time.*

*He spent most of the days and nights in prayer and it
seemed that God must have been in the room standing
beside him from the way he looked.*

*Everyone has been wonderful to me . . . an Irish nurse, a
Dutch nurse, a Russian refugee doctor, an English major
and his wife and many others. Of course the mission family
was exceptionally wonderful. Dr. & Mrs. Christy almost
never left me. Dr. Christy did a great deal of the nursing
care himself and sat with him for hours and hours on end.*

*Funerals here are on the same day as the death if at all
possible so the funeral was at six o'clock last night. Our
church, which holds about 200, was far too small so we had
it on the lawn in front of the church. I have no idea how
many people were there. Mac had friends from every walk
of life out here. He was greatly loved by those who were
Christians as well as by those who were not. The casket was
made by members of the staff and was covered and lined
with white satin. His face was as sweet as could be. Besides
a number of cars there were two big busses . . . one from the
cement factory and one from the ordnance factory.*

Dorothy Christy remarked that as she looked at one bench

she saw a hardened Muslim, one Muslim not quite so hard, the Catholic priest, a Muslim convert who is a college professor, a British army major etc. There were most if not all the English people from the ordnance factory. They all loved him very much tho' they are very much people of this world and he never pulled any punches in preaching. They came again and again to hear him.

There were Muslims from the nearby villages.

But the people he loved most of all were there in large numbers . . . the raggle-taggle looking sweepers and laborers from several places, humble Christian people to whom he preached and whom he was always ready to help.

Missionaries drove from over 150 miles away through the terrific heat.

The service was wonderful . . . both in English and Urdu. The congregation sang one of Mac's favorite songs 'Jesus, Lover of my Soul.' A young missionary couple with beautiful voices sang 'He the Pearly Gates Will Open.' As they sang in the evening light I could just see those gates open to let Mac in.

How I wish you could all have known him better!

Now what to do? My heart is, of course, here. This quickly became home and will always be so now. I would like to spend my life here as Mac wanted to spend his here. I can carry on a good bit of his work. He did many things that I can look after and keep going. Dr. Christy has several ideas for me . . . one is to take over the business management of the hospital and continue with evangelistic work. What will develop I don't know. First I would like to go home to you for a while. The summer is unbearable here because of the heat, and I don't want to go to our vacation place alone . . . I couldn't bear that. I should be able to leave by air next

*week if I can get passage and necessary papers. I would like
to come back again in the fall. I will let you know definitely
as soon as my thoughts get straightened out.*

*Frances, will you please pass this letter on to the church and
to members of the family.*

Much love,
Marie

(In England a young engineer happens to spot that same week
an advertisement in an unfamiliar newspaper. It looks for a civil
engineer to work in Pakistan and he writes a letter of inquiry. It
will lead to work in a factory adjacent to Taxila Hospital.)

Marie McGuill

Back to Taxila - Alone
October 1953

Strangely, as soon as Marie reaches New York and Maynard, Mac's brother, and his wife Crete meet her at La Guardia, she knows for certain that this land, her birthplace, is not where home is for her anymore. Something has happened to her in just four years. She feels opposite to the way she had felt when she had returned from Italy after the war. She isn't needed here; she is out of place, a stranger visiting. The Big City for her now is the dusty colonial city of Rawalpindi whose streets are still almost bare of private cars and filled instead with tongas (two wheeled horse taxi carts), bicycles and pedestrians. Her Statue of Liberty has become the great narrow yellow bulk of Massey Gate funneling the traffic toward the station and beyond.

Somehow in these short, short years with Mac home has become for her Taxila, the hospital, the patients, the several languages—she is fluent in Urdu and can make sense of Pushtu and Punjabi—the hustle and bustle, the smells, the spices, the bazars, and the traffic, the buses, the tongas and the closed level crossing as trains crowded with passengers rattle through slowing down for the station.

The half of the house she has shared with Mac that they have created together on the Mission Compound is now really home. It is the only place she can call home or even wants to call home. Dorothy has thought as she sees the young widow off at Rawalpindi that Marie does not know what she will do when she gets back to the States but behind the shock in Marie's own mind there have been no doubts—Taxila is calling. She will need to get back before long. Her memories are there, they have reality. There will be more to create when she gets back. Her help will be needed for the eye season that will begin as soon as the heat is over and patients come out of the mountains and valleys on their way by rail or bus to Taxila. Dorothy's baby is due at the end of September and she will try to be back for that. She can cover then for Dorothy in the operating room.

Where she can, she will pick up and carry on Mac's work. Although she will be mainly working among the women she'll also be, with the two Bible women, encouraging Gulab Khan, the pastor at Taxila, in every way possible.

More important is Wah, their immediate neighbor, growing into a city before their eyes, there needs to be movement in establishing a congregation that will grow to meet the needs of the Protestant Christians of the city. Mac and she have started working among the new arrivals, the sweepers and the laborers and their families, as soon as construction on the dwellings for workers has progressed to some occupancy. Mac has seen that one day this group of Christians, likely to number ultimately several thousands, will need pastoral care and that a church building will be needed for their nurture and worship. It is too much for Padri Gulab to try to fill Mac's work with the men over there. Even before Mac died they have been corresponding with Wilbur whether any student graduating from the Seminary might be suitable for the Wah work. The seeds of the women's work are flourishing; it is almost ahead of the men's work. The literacy classes are waiting to be picked up as soon as she gets back. This summer away will be enough.

Mac's family has been so loving, so thoughtful. Later she flies on to Lundy in San Jose in California and up to Selah for time with Frances. How can any of them understand, even as they talk, why she can only think of getting back to Taxila? For them Taxila spells tragedy, for her it is and will always be home.

Patiently, gently they allow Marie to unfold the story of what has happened. She decorates their limited picture with stories about Mac's humor, his jokes and fun, his singing, his preaching, his vision, his work not only among the patients and the staff but also in his English preaching on Sunday evenings.

They find the story of Mac's developing ministry to the foreigners, mainly British, who work at Wah Ordnance Factory intriguing. She explains—

> *In the beginning Pakistan has few factories. Almost all the industrial infrastructure of India lies to the east of the line dividing the Punjab. Where are the simple everyday things like tires, nails, nuts and bolts going to come from*

now? But the fledgling government is most desperate over its slender defenses, viewing India from which it has separated the potential enemy.

Pakistan indeed has some weapons left behind as its share of the resources of the old Indian Army but little means of increasing them by manufacture or purchase. A war with India could erupt at any time and, for all the courage that might be shown, without weapons it can only be a matter of time.

A high proportion of its budget, so needed to create a societal framework, will have to go in the early years on obtaining weapons and creating and maintaining at readiness large defense forces.

So it is that Pakistan's major initial industrial investment is the creation of an ordnance factory and accommodations for its workers. It is located a good distance from the Indian border, along the Grand Trunk Road that has crossed for centuries, even millennia, northern India from Calcutta into the Khyber Pass and Afghanistan. The location chosen is a flat undeveloped plain west of the Margalla hills and to the east of Wah, a village between Hasan Abdal and Taxila which has a plentiful supply of fresh spring water.

Initially no sophisticated weapons are produced, just bullets, shells, guns, rifles and mines. The British Government is supplying requested expertise from its own Royal Ordnance Factories. Up to a hundred foreigners and their families are resident in two messes for single men and bungalows for the families. They will be there for another decade.

Mac has been the chaplain for the Protestants among them. He sees their need and isn't one to let a vacuum be unchallenged. The Britishers love him. He speaks plainly and preaches persuasively. He visits, he counsels, he condoles, he encourages. He lives what he speaks. They see it and love it. This is a Christianity they can empathize with, enjoy and be challenged by. Here is a man whose relationship with Jesus has not formality but vitality. In the homes of the missionary staff of the hospital they find welcome and hospitality, friendship and Christian example. They see it is possible to be a servant within a position of authority. They glimpse what life can be like when the drive of personal ambition is removed from a situation and all are content to be equals. And they enjoy meeting Americans that don't fit the stereotypes—who invite them to tea.

Each Sunday evening, even during the summer, an ordnance factory bus picks up Mac's English congregation and brings them to Taxila. Marie and Mac share their rooms with another nurse having set aside one room of their home for a chapel. Later, after the new chapel building is finished, the small congregation is able to move there but the single foreigners particularly miss the interchanges, and the refreshments, after the service that the house chapel has made possible.

Norval is at the airport in Chaklala, Rawalpindi together with the two American nurses to meet Marie when in early October she arrives back from her journey to the States. There is a lot of news to share. Dorothy has had Joanne a week or so previously and both are doing well. OA is down with hepatitis so things have been hectic.

There are tears to be shed, hugs to be exchanged. Everything is going to be so different, but as the news begins to flow of the staff changes, of the marriages and the pregnancies and the babies and the deaths and the events of the hot season in Murree and Taxila, the pain eases.

The late rains have delayed the eye season for a few days but patients are already beginning to come and tomorrow they will be starting at 5:30 am.

Norval has recovered the luggage and they are on their way to Qamran's for a cup of tea and Esajee's for the shopping before they head out of Pindi into the setting sun. There are so many things to catch up with on the twenty-two mile journey up the Grand Trunk Road past Nicholson's monument to Serai Kala and Taxila.

It is good to be home.

There is a sad little item in the June 1953 minutes of the Executive Committee of the Sialkot mission. Marie has just left for the States after Mac's death and it is not known whether she will return:

> 502 (6) If Mrs. H.J. McGuill applies for reappointment as either missionary or associate missionary, we recommend that the Board consider her application favorably.

It is both an invitation and a hope from the field that she will come back to Pakistan and to them.

At Annual Meeting time that same year, Marie is just back in Taxila from the States. She is hesitant to go down to Sialkot to meet the whole assembled Mission while she is beginning to pick up the threads of her life. She isn't sure she can handle the emotional stress that will be involved.

In addition, Taxila Hospital has to be serviced with staff and kept running. You can close down schools but not hospitals. Dorothy has her new baby and the two other single nurses, Flo Carithers and Mary Lentz, are off to Sialkot. There is no easy way Marie can go but the Mission takes the following action about her, delighted that she has come back:

That Mrs. H.J. McGuill be located in Taxila, to occupy her former apartment with the exception of the office. That she be requested to do evangelistic and adult literacy work in Taxila and Wah Cantonment.

Although she is an exceptionally fine nurse, the Mission knows and is sensitive to her desire to perpetuate Mac's own work.

We can assume that Marie has applied to the Women's Board of Foreign Missions for appointment as a full member of the Sialkot Mission. Without doubt Hawthorne Gospel Church in New Jersey would have been willing and happy to continue her financial support.

Christmas in the Desert

1954

Marie is one of the three single nurses at Taxila, a likeable and friendly woman in her early forties. She has returned from America to her work at the hospital not long after I arrive in Wah in August of 1953. My fellow travelers on the church bus have told me about the tragic loss of her husband from polio at the beginning of the summer. He had been their pastor and they had dearly loved him.

She has been at the regular Sunday evening services at Taxila chapel and also at occasional special events on the Mission Compound. She and Dr. Brown have been at pains to invite me to a conference of Frontier missionaries in February the following year. She thought I might be interested, and has made sure I felt welcome when I turn up in the evenings after work is done.

Late in April I receive instructions to close down my work in Wah and get down to Hyderabad in Sindh Province as quickly as possible. A cement factory needs to be completed several miles outside the city on the Badin road. It has already been started but has run into problems.

At the end of April, three selected workmen and I set off from Wah to drive south about eight hundred miles, non-stop if possible, through the Thal desert and on to Hyderabad. We are taking the most direct route which means we travel on the worst roads.

In November of 1954 I am surprised to hear from Marie that she is coming to Hyderabad and there might be opportunity to meet.

This is something to look forward to; I have enjoyed my interlude in Wah and my contacts at the hospital. It will be a break from the daily grind at the cement factory to have a visitor from Taxila.

Marie is to be the housekeeper for a team of literacy experts coming to advise the Provincial Government of Sindh. The leader is a world famous missionary pioneer of literacy, Dr. Frank Laubach. Marie has been using his methods in her own literacy work in Wah and she is looking forward to the opportunity to work with him.

At Hyderabad, the old capital of the Sindh Government, they will be staying at the Canal Rest Houses. Marie has told me the date they will be arriving early in December and I drive down to the city to check that there are no initial problems they might need help with. My car has no windshield, I have had an encounter with a bullock cart, dead center, and windshields are just not available but no matter.

Is Marie glad to see me! I think if she hadn't been a missionary she might even have kissed me! She and six others have come up by morning train from Karachi, have taken *tongas*, three of them, to the Canal Rest Houses. They have been firmly told as soon as they arrive that their confirmed reservations have been cancelled by the Sindh Government. The chief minister has called an emergency meeting of his cabinet in Hyderabad.

The principal of the local college has come also to welcome them and he will take Dr. Laubach and his wife but that is all he can take.

Marie's thought of a local hotel gives me shudders. There is only one to consider. I have stayed there on my first arrival. That is no place for any foreign woman, especially the two with Marie who are strangers to Pakistan. Come to think of it, it is no place for the two men either. In fact I'm not sure it is a place where any foreigner should stay.

No, they should all come and stay with me and Stuart. I will go and make arrangements and be back in two hours or so to pick them up. Just relax, arrange some tea, everything will be all right. No, no trouble at all.

Well, not much, anyway. I hurry into the pottery and cloth bazars on my way home to buy dishes and cutlery, a couple of tablecloths and bedding—quilts and sheets and pillows. I totally forget curtains.

I pick up a load of vegetables, all kinds of tinned foods, several pounds of loose porridge, local brown sugar and powdered milk.

At the house I am giving instructions to the cook who hasn't changed the menu for six months. Get another block of ice fast. Americans like their water cold. His eyes are rolling.

I jam a paintbrush into Stuart's hand and tell him to start painting the panes of glass in the bedroom. Fortunately it is white paint. He is swilling the paint around so generously it is obvious that when it is all over we will have to replace the panes of glass if we want to see out. We only have two rooms, a bedroom and a dining / living room. The women will have the bedroom and the men will sleep out on the verandah.

I am off to pick up the guests as I ask Stuart to please make sure the living room is tidy. And put some of those horrible yellow periwinkles from the garden in a jam jar or two. Stick them in the women's bedroom to help them feel at home.

I am finding Marie's hospital background useful. She is obviously a very competent nurse and there are many medical emergencies on a busy construction site. She doesn't really like giving me advice as to what medications to use but I wheedle it out of her.

By Christmas only Marie and Chesley, the authoress, are left. The training program has been completed, the Laubach team has dispersed but Taxila is too far for Marie and Chesley to get home before Christmas. They are spending Christmas with us.

We attend services in an old Victorian Gothic brick church. Father Lavery, an Anglican missionary, serves communion and it makes the day really feel like Christmas Day. After church we are invited to have lunch with a Danish family who lives in the neighborhood.

The piece de resistance is yet to come—Allah Buksh's Christmas dinner. He has been working all day at it. His face beams with every triumphal dish delivered. Our table decor has never looked better. On a great platter, cooked to a turn (how did he do it?) is a glorious roasted bird. It's not a chicken or even a turkey!

"What's that, Allah Buksh?"

In his limited accented English he explains, bursting with pride, "It is duck."

Stuart and I both blanch. We only know of one duck, our pet Donald! We look at Donald with sadness and a distinct loss of appetite and ask Hagen if he will please carve the poultry.

The day after Boxing Day I put Marie and Chesley into the overcrowded women's compartment of the Tez Gam express at Hyderabad.

Hagen drops in to visit after they have gone and, out of the blue, makes a strange remark. "Why don't you marry Marie, Ken?"

I laugh, caught totally by surprise "Oh, she's far older than I am." But the question lingers.

Marie Writes to Freda

February 2, 1955

Dear Freda,

I spent the first part of December in Karachi and then went with the Laubach team 135 miles into the desert to the city of Hyderabad. There the team had some work to do in the Sindhi language. Since they didn't finish until Christmas

Eve and home was 1000 miles away I stayed on there. Pakistan is not really the place to spend Christmas.

I had a friend there who had been a member of our church here in Taxila and who had been kind enough to take in some team members while they were working in that area so one of the team members, Mrs. Chesley Baity, a writer of children's books, and I stayed.

On Christmas morning we went to a tumbling down Church of England for the morning service. Since the English have gone many of their churches are falling apart. The draperies were in shreds, the doors wouldn't close, bits were gone from the windows, the roof was in bad shape but the service was lovely in spite of the dust. There were about a dozen people, mostly English, and it was a communion service.

After church we did a bit of sight seeing. Then we went to visit a Danish family who were neighbors of our host. Then went back to our own host's house—a two-room adobe shack on a construction site for dinner. The house was most cozy. Dinner guests were a Danish engineer, an English couple who are now Canadian citizens, the American writer, myself, another English engineer and our host, also an English engineer.

After dinner we sat out in the sun in the walled courtyard talking about our missions in life, eating nuts, candy, fruit, cake and drinking tea until the sun went down. We were right out in the desert so as soon as the sun went down it got cold.

We moved into the house to sit before the fireplace and listened to classical music played by the Dane on the record player.

It would have been interesting to know the thoughts of all of us as we gazed into the fire for a couple of hours without anyone saying anything. Up until a very short time before we had all been strangers. We were all far from home.

After supper our host gave Christmas presents from the makeshift Christmas tree. Mine was a box of Yardleys soap from our host and his assistant engineer. Then we sat before the fire again and listened to more music until bedtime.

All in all it was a most interesting and unusual Christmas.

Marie

Does she have any inkling that within a year she will be married to her British host; the man who lives in a two-room adobe hut on a construction site? Or that she is heading towards becoming mother of more than fifty daughters in the orphanage she has recently left in Karachi?

The Year In-between

It is nearing mid-September in 1955. It has been a long hard hot summer. There are four of us foreigners working on the cement factory project, sometimes five. It is going well. We have caught up with the backlog and are frequently waiting for drawings.

I receive a phone call from Karachi. It is the Managing Director. The company has received a contract for the construction of the Dry Dock in Karachi. I am being transferred there as Chief Engineer. Yes, he knows the work in Hyderabad isn't finished but I should hand over within the week and get on down to Karachi.

He tells me I can fly home to England for a couple of weeks rest as soon as the accounts are all sorted out in a month or so. A month seems to me at that time about as long as a century. I can't wait that long, I'm done in. I'll just go up to the Punjab for a break and then come down to Karachi.

I reckon later that I must have been suffering from heat stroke to turn down an offer for a flight home to England because I wasn't willing to wait for a month. Either that or I was unknowingly keeping a divine appointment and, in addition, going on a tour that would show me in the next couple of weeks almost all the places that would fill the next thirty-five years of my life.

I send a telegram and a letter to Taxila Hospital asking if they can accommodate an exhausted engineer from Hyderabad for a couple of weeks. I am sure Marie will be happy to arrange return hospitality if it is possible.

The train journey of twenty-four hours from Hyderabad to Taxila is refreshing. I am looking forward to seeing Marie again. She meets me at Taxila station. She has a little 500cc Fiat Popolino. Into it we dump the luggage and then maneuver ourselves in.

I am surprised to be met and to see how pleased she is to see me. I have not remembered that lovely smile that lights up her whole face.

She has news. There are problems in the nursing school at Sialkot Hospital and she has been asked to transfer there as Nursing Matron. She will be going at the end of the week. She is not going by rail, she will take the car and no one will accompany her. I arrange to travel with her as escort, it wouldn't be safe for a woman to be traveling alone on a journey of close to two hundred miles and besides—I've never seen Sialkot. Marie seems pleased with the arrangement.

The days pass pleasantly; Marie drives me out to the building sites where I had worked in Wah. Something is happening to both of us that we have not planned on or even dreamt of when we met at the station. I am realizing that Marie is a beautiful woman and it is not just her smile, she has further an inner radiance and strength that previously somehow I've missed. We are falling in love. There are so many good reasons why it should not be so. There is an age difference of almost eleven years. I definitely am not a missionary *type* and have little desire to be one. Marie is committed to her missionary life in Pakistan. Also I am English and Marie is American—we are still laughing over the differences between us forty years later.

It is Marie's last day in Taxila. The manager of the cement factory has invited Marie to a farewell dinner and graciously includes me as her guest.

That afternoon I kneel down in my room and talk to God about the strange thing that is happening to me. I have promised God can have the rest of my life. I meant that. But does it fit within His will for me that I ask Marie to marry me? If Gideon could put out a fleece then I can too. I am going to a reception tonight and I want Him to stop the car right in front of the shisham tree that is thirty yards short of Gilani's garage. If that happens then I'll know. I need to know for sure.

If Gideon could put out a fleece on the threshing floor beneath the oak tree at Ophrah in order to make sure he understood God's will then I could put out my fleece at the shisham tree in Taxila.

It is a late dinner and already dark when we leave. Marie is driving the Popolino. If she had measured with a tape she could not have stopped suddenly more accurately in front of the shisham tree thirty yards short of Gilani's garage. She has a strange feeling the rear lights aren't working. I get out to check but I know I don't need to. The lights are okay and I can sense God is smiling.

When I propose to Marie she hesitates and asks whether

there are not others I should check with first? I tell her I have
already checked, and besides, I am of age. There is another
moment or so of silence and then that lovely smile and an answer
in the affirmative.

Wedding Bells

December 29, 1955

Marie has chosen our wedding date while she is visiting Karachi to see where she will be living. The wedding will be at Taxila. She will go back from Sialkot to Taxila as soon as she has gathered her things together and handed over the work. I will fly up from Karachi just before Christmas.

She stays with Marian Laugesen at the Orphanage. I collect her each day after work. She has borrowed a bathing suit from the most recent young arrival to the Sialkot Mission who is doing

language study with the Fosters at CTI. By driving out beyond
Hawkes Bay to the west of Karachi, we can find a totally secluded
beach lapped by blue waters and bathed with the November sun.
These are a few halcyon days.

Marie makes all the wedding arrangements with Dorothy's
willing help. Everyone, or almost everyone on the hospital staff
who has known Marie and Mac together, wants to help. It is more
than most could have hoped for that their beloved Sister McGuill
is re-finding the happiness she has lost so tragically just two and
a half years ago.

Only two have hesitations. Khan Zaman, her servant, is uneasy,
deeply uneasy. Had his mistress been marrying another missionary
he would have had no trouble. He could even have overlooked my
unfortunate nationality if I had been a missionary but I am both
English *and not* a missionary! He *knows* how Englishmen treated
their wives. What ever will happen to this defenseless woman he
loves so much once I get her away to Karachi and can beat her to
my heart's content?

OA is also uneasy. He likes me as a person, we play chess
together, but spiritually I am way out in deep field! I argue over
plain-as-a-pikestaff Scripture and doctrine. I am well meaning
but there is little depth to my spiritual understanding. I am a one-
off still awaiting a work of grace in my heart. He hesitates to discuss this matter with Marie who is obviously so happy, surely she
has sorted this out with me somewhere along the courtship route
but he isn't sure enough to be at total ease about it. He makes it a
matter of prayer.

When I ask Dorothy Christy why she, Marie's closest friend
and matron of honor, has allowed Marie to marry such a suspect
character as I am she blithely replies, "Oh, I had no doubts on that
score. She so obviously is in love with you, that is enough. I just
wonder how you will work out the difference in your ages."

The Sialkot Mission has been deeply affected by Mac's death. He was greatly loved without exception. The Mission had been a family in tears. Now the members of that family have occasion and opportunity to rejoice with Marie even though her husband-to-be is an unknown quantity. From all over the Punjab they come to Taxila on December 29th.

Stuart, my fellow site engineer at the cement factory in Hyderabad, has flown up from Karachi the previous day to be the best man. He is quite at ease with missionaries by this time and organizes a very necessary protection against missionary pranks of the little Fiat Popolino we are planning to drive away to Rawalpindi later on in the day.

Padri Gulab Khan, the wonderful old Taxila pastor and Uncle Willie Sutherland, Mac's dear friend and mentor, share the service. The weather is one of those wonderful dry crisp cool days of winter just before the onset of the winter rains. The reception is on the lawn of Marie's previous home against a backdrop wall of poinsettias eight feet tall.

Although I think I am taking Marie away from Taxila for good, she sees her departure in different terms. God will bring her back to Taxila in His own good time and her new husband will be linked in service with her.

The Gift of a Home

January 1956

We arrive in Karachi on the last day of the year, flying down from Rawalpindi. I had left the car at the airport and now, approaching midnight, I am bringing my new wife home to the house in Mauripur on the west side of Karachi that Ian Hibble had built for himself and his wife some years earlier.

I am soon to discover that my life is going to be radically benefited by my marriage to this woman whom I hardly know. The eight months we live in Mauripur I work on the Karachi Dry

Dock and the State Bank Building. Marie and I are adjusting to each other, not changing each other to a more common mean but learning more about each other. We laugh a lot during the process. We are so different.

When I marry Marie I have little or no background in the staples Christians enjoy privately and between each other. Marie leads a devout life shared with others. She has personal devotions, attends prayer meetings and finds time for Bible Study.

My religious journey has essentially been a solitary one. I enjoy my times with God although they are frequently more argumentative than reflective. I am now being inducted into a new world where people recognize fellowship as a discipline designed for spiritual growth. Bible Study is an enjoyable activity where people from a variety of backgrounds but with a common interest meet together regularly to study Scripture. This is a refreshing, almost exciting, discovery.

While waiting to marry Marie during the end months of 1955 I accept the invitation of a Methodist missionary to attend the weekly Bible Study at the manse in Garden Road in Karachi. Roughly a dozen people attend—American, Canadian, British, Anglo-Pakistani and Pakistani. There is lively and knowledgeable discussion and by no means uniformity of understanding or views. These lay people—engineers, bankers, accountants, clerks and housewives know their Bibles far better than I. There is, I observe with surprise, a great deal of room to differ and no discord or dogmatism expressed. Interesting! I have been thinking all Christians are supposed to believe in and subscribe to exactly the same beliefs. Why, even though there is not a remote chance that I might squeeze in under the bar it is becoming clear the barrier is not as impenetrable as I have supposed.

Unexpectedly Hoyt Smith asks me one Thursday to lead the Bible Study; we are studying the latter chapters of Isaiah. That is very trusting; doesn't he see from the questions I've been asking that I am an obvious heretic? People are very kind, they say the views I express are *refreshing*.

(I have observed that when Americans are faced directly with the question whether something is jolly good or brutally awful they choose for the latter answer the euphemism *very interesting*. *Refreshing* is of the same standard of reply but just slightly milder.)

Not only is marriage to Marie opening doors to a deeper spiritual life for me, I am becoming aware of a woman who brings warmth and welcome into the very heart of a home.

I, a site engineer accustomed to living basically, am not only embarking on the adventure of married life with all its adjustments. I am being taken into the school of domesticity and being shown by a superb practitioner the art of home building. I never met anyone else who is more capable of turning a house, a home, into a reflection of her own personality than Marie. Within minutes, with a reordering of a piece of furniture, a rose in a bud vase, a window open, a curtain adjusted and a floor covering moved things would begin to happen and a house begin to live.

I have met many gifted women whose homes represent their personalities. Generally I have observed that the homes of old style nurses, those who really know how to nurse, are shining and spotless and well ordered. Hospital life teaches them that.

I have known other women, each possessing a far more beautiful home, whose furniture is elegant and who is totally mistress of the arts of hospitality. None of them has ever matched Marie as a homemaker or as a hostess although Marie's furniture has just about always been secondhand.

Marie has a gift. Her home is an extension of herself. She shares her home just as she shares herself, unstintingly. She is always neat and trim. So is her house. She is happy and relaxed, so is her home. She isn't creating something temporary even though in our first five years of married life we change homes seventeen times. Wherever she is really is home for her and each receives her imprint. Her home is the forum where she expresses her stewardship. It is the way she gives thanks to God for His goodness to her, the way she shares unconsciously the Good News, the way she eases the loneliness of others.

Having English tea in bone china teacups always helps!

She is also continuing the pattern of her remarkable household—having guests continually throughout much of her married life. One or two stay for years, many stay for months at a time. This had begun as soon as Mac and she had arrived back in Taxila six years previously. There she had an active life helping her husband in his work as the hospital evangelist while she was working as a nurse in the same hospital. In addition, she naturally moved to share the burden of hospitality that every Mission Station experiences. What helped make it possible to turn her home into a caravanserai was her remarkable servant that she had acquired along with her marriage. More of him later.

It is not that Marie is always ready for guests. She prefers them to come after 7 a.m. and before 9 p.m. It is always better if they don't come while she is taking her hour's rest after lunch and especially not on Sunday afternoons. However, people do come at these inconvenient times and she will make them welcome. She tells me that once Mac had been called in the middle of the night from the hospital, a patient he had met was calling for him. Mac deferred his response until he rose at dawn but the patient had died meanwhile. Mac had never forgiven himself. She remembers that. One must be ready to respond as and when the need arises.

Once, when we are living in a Punjabi city with many missionaries engaged in all kinds of work, a Pakistani Christian colleague takes me by surprise with the comment "You know, there are two missionaries here who do not love us!" I laugh at the absurdity. He gives me the names of the two he is thinking of. I recognize immediately, with surprise, that he is right. One is a man and the other a woman. They work in different institutions. While their spouses do truly love Pakistanis they, although they are both attractive in personality, don't really love the nationals they live amongst. The criteria my friend is judging them by is simple. "When we come to the door they do not invite us in." This though is merely a symptom that shows.

We once, in the late eighties, in Gujranwala have a charming young American girl as a volunteer. Candi has everything worked out. Now that she has her degree she is going to make a career in computers. Her marriage will be a partnership and this will be sorted out before the marriage or else it will not take place. The careers of both partners will be equally important. When babies come along, there will only be one or two of course; she and her husband will decide mutually whose career is going to be put on the back burner for a while. It will as likely be the husband's as the wife's.

We are amused at the strange ideas of young people but not so amused when we realize that we are the ones out of tune. She is speaking not for herself but for a whole generation—a lost generation. Maybe more than one generation.

For Marie her fulfillment lies in the very ideas that Candi so resolutely rejects. She counts being a good wife and a good homemaker a privilege her sex allows her. Her Aunt Ida in Selah had shown her what a fulfilled woman could be, bringing into the domain of her home the Christian standards she lived by and then turning them into opportunities. Marie is a superb nurse but nursing is only her profession. She gladly puts it aside for the richer lifetime career of being a wife, a mother and a homemaker. Her missionary effectiveness does not stem from her nursing but from the home she creates, the way she uses it and the character that develops in her as she does so.

I used to hate the summers when the boys were in school in Murree and Marie, from late May until early September, had to be up in the hills creating a home for them there. Down on the plains in Sialkot or Gujranwala or in Taxila her home in summer would shrivel and die for the life, her life, had gone out of it. The dust would fall; the birds nested in the cornices, the refrigerator would be virtually empty. No flowers sang from the vases. Marie had mastered the art of using doors, windows and curtains to control the heat in the house. When the outside temperature was higher everything was closed up, when cooler everything was open. Not while she was away, though.

When we leave Gujranwala forty-three years after she has first come to Pakistan she leaves without a sigh her home and almost all its accumulated treasures of association. She leaves the pictures, books, linens, furniture and utensils for the benefit of whoever will follow her in the house. The guest book, filled with hundreds of names, a diary of the saints, this is one treasure she takes with her.

I am also observing something else that is interesting about being married—it will lead, and continue to lead, to an enlarging family. What's so surprising about that, you may ask. It is the usual thing that happens to married couples. However it isn't like that with us. It is almost as though there is a God-agenda taking place, bringing our lives into mesh with others that He is also interested in.

It is strange the way God works in this area. It is as though we are the nucleus of an atom and in a constant process little electrons spinning off on their own into space suddenly accrue to the nucleus and change occurs and the enlargement continues.

In Marie's and my case we seem to gather children almost from the beginning. First there are our sixty children at the orphanage in Karachi who naturally call us Momma and Poppa. There is Lilian who now lives in Italy. Then there is a seven week only baby boy wriggling in his cot at Birdhurst Lodge in Croydon whom we call Timmy. Then a little four-year old ginger haired brother for him called Colin. Later come our boys at the Technical Training Centre in Gujranwala who again call Marie Momma but elevate my status to Baba, Grandfather. Over time come Munawar and his family and then three further daughters. Some of these new family members you will read about later.

In John Haines' covering letter to excerpts from his diary that I quote elsewhere he speaks for many:

> *I take this opportunity to thank you for giving me the chance to work and live with you and your family – these are some of the most special memories I have. You have no idea what an impact you made on my life!*
>
> *I will always remember Marie: the Mother, the nurse, the devoted wife, your right (and left) hand, the LADY in charge of the house – watching over everything from groceries to laundry – and the one person I let down when I wasn't at the dinner table on time (I was in the process of splicing a telephone cable with two different sets of color codes and had them in my head when she came after me about dinner. I knew if I left the splicing it would take me half a morning to figure out what I had done.)*
>
> *I was and am in admiration of her getting up at 2 a.m. during the height of the cataract season. The world lost a saint when Heaven reclaimed her. I think the thing I most admired about her was the fact that from Day One I didn't feel a visitor but part of her family!*

Marie will recreate her home, the brightness, its friendliness and its openness twelve thousand miles away in Richland. Then, finally three years later, halfway back again in Sellindge, England.

Marie has been finding leisure in Karachi a distinct adjustment after a life committed to caring for others or studying. For a short while immediately after her marriage she is a housewife with no other responsibilities except her husband and her home.

She is not finding time weighing on her hands however. She is an assiduous correspondent. Over her life in Pakistan I estimate she has written over fifty thousand letters. She has a gift of acquiring and then maintaining friendships. She is genuinely interested in people and their families. Her letters, conversational in manner, pick up where she has left off and continue chatting. She corresponds for decades with people from churches in the States whom she never meets.

There is however going to be little time ahead for leisure.

Zeb and Marie

Khan Zaman

January – August 1956

The house at Mauripur on the western edge of Karachi provides a brief but delightful setting to the start of our married life together. Marie becomes engrossed in transforming it into a home. The presence of Khan Zaman makes this easier for her.

When Marie married Mac, she was probably only just aware that she was getting two great men rather than one in her marriage. It would have been easy for her to forget on her late summer honeymoon in the Pocono Mountains of Pennsylvania, in a cabin on the edge of a lake, that waiting for them both when they returned to Taxila was the Jeeves to her husband's Wooster. Well, not quite. Mac was certainly no Wooster but certainly KZ had many of the qualities of Jeeves.

Khan Zaman observes with some curiosity the woman, a stranger, who has accompanied Mac on his visit back to Taxila for those couple of days at Christmas in 1947. He has noticed Mac's happiness and his animation. He wonders with his wife, Mir Jan, whether perhaps there is a marriage arrangement in the making and whether Dr. Karsgaard will become involved. He has suggested to Mac before he leaves for home from Campbellpur that someone, perhaps his brother, might make an arrangement for him so that he can come back with a wife to help take care of him. Mac just laughs; God will be making his arrangement, all in good time. KZ would have liked to talk with the woman, she is friendly and approachable, but she speaks no Urdu and his English is limited. Miss McConnell just shrugs her shoulders. She too is curious but has no answers.

Khan Zaman has little experience of working for Englishmen. All his experiences of foreigners have been with American missionaries. When missionary families go on furlough the normal practice is that they make arrangements for their servants to work temporarily with friends until they return. Usually this is with other missionaries. It is a custom that works very well. Missionaries understand the code and did not try to develop loyalties that will seduce the good servant away from his furloughing employer.

On one occasion only had Khan Zaman worked for an Englishman. He was a Superintendent of Police and obviously not a missionary by type. He smoked and he drank and he beat his wife. (My guess would be if he were to be consistent, he also beat his servants.)

Khan Zaman has formed several strongly held opinions from his experiences. No Americans drink or smoke or beat their wives. All Englishmen drink and smoke and beat their wives.

Khan Zaman is a man of intense loyalties.

When Mac was dying, the doctors were concerned that the polio not be transmitted to others for the manner of transmission of infection was uncertain. Particularly they were concerned for Khan Zaman who had half a dozen young children. He would have none of it. His place was at the side of Mac. He had also by now included Marie in his total loyalties and he needed to be with her also. Electricity failures were a commonplace. Who would be there to manually operate the iron lung pump? Who else had a right to operate it if it were not Khan Zaman? Norval yielded to his insistence and the vigils were shared until the end.

Now to his great concern, if not his dismay, his beloved Memsahiba is marrying an Englishman and, to make matters worse, not even a missionary. He is sure to beat her. How can this have happened? Does she not know? Has she become blind?

When she returns to Taxila to prepare for the wedding planned for just after Christmas he can hardly bear the thought of the disaster ahead of her. Who will take care of her? He announces to her that he will accompany her to Karachi. He will leave his family behind in the Punjab but she will not be able to manage without him, it is his duty and he will come down by train. He has never been to Karachi. His daughter, Zeba, will write a letter telling when he will arrive.

Marie, and I as well, are delighted to have Khan Zaman although she has not anticipated his coming. Wali Mohammed, my own servant, who has been steadily taking me for a ride, decides to ride with someone else when my astute and fluent house manager takes over checking the shopping and the accounts. Men are easy to work for, women are much more difficult.

The guests of the newly married couple are now beginning to arrive.

These are first Stuart and then Hagen and his wife, Ruth,

who has arrived to join her husband in Hyderabad. There are also occasional Sialkot Mission friends in transit and new missionaries associated with various missions that Marie is asked to meet and send upcountry after their luggage is cleared through customs.

Khan Zaman is in his element cooking for and caring for his missionary friends. He shrugs his shoulders, spreads his hands and says, "I can't teach, I can't preach but with these hands I can minister to those who can and do."

Since it is Khan Zaman's first opportunity to see the sea we take him down to a ship, a freighter, that has brought a missionary couple we are meeting. We are permitted to take him on board. He wanders over the ship with curiosity but he is not impressed. He had seen such vessels on the Dal Lake in Srinagar in Kashmir!

We take him out to Hawkes Bay and drive past the evaporating pools where white cones of salt have been gathered after evaporation has occurred. He is doubtful of our explanation but says nothing. At the beach he runs his toes through the sand and asks, "I suppose THIS is brown sugar."

We almost have a tragedy when Marie, Stuart and I go swimming at Sandspit. The undertow on the steep beach is treacherous and fierce. Marie gets into trouble first and although she is a good swimmer she cannot get back. I am nearby and try to help her. She cries out despairingly "Save yourself, I can't make it!" Desperately, with the last of my strength, I throw her onto a large wave that bursts over us and she is carried by it to a point where her toes touch the sand. She scrambles up the slope and I after her. We both lie for a while breathless and exhausted face down on the sand, still lapped by water, realizing we have faced death a moment only away. Stuart is even further out but a stronger swimmer than either of us. We wave madly. He turns back and struggles for the shore.

Marie doesn't go swimming again because, mysteriously, her

bathing suit disappears from the clothesline on which it is hang-
ing to dry after rinsing the salt out. A curious theft that. Nothing
else is missing. We never find out who took it but I personally
suspected that a loyal servant was trying to keep his Memsahiba
out of harm's way the only way he knew how.

Several months have passed. Khan Zaman announces to us at
breakfast that the Karachi water has no strength in it and that he
has decided for the sake of his own health it will be necessary for
him to return to the Punjab. We smile at each other and at him.
We all know without discussing it. I have passed the test. I do not
drink. I do not smoke. I do not beat my wife. I have achieved the
American standard. He can trust Marie to me *and* I also am now
co-sharer with Marie of his loyalty.

He comes back to us again when we return to the Punjab but
many things are to happen before that event occurs.

January 24, 1972

On Tuesday a troubled old man with not much longer left makes
his way from the hospital to the telephone office in Taxila. When
he hears my voice he cannot speak for emotion. The operator,
who knows everybody's business, gives the message for him,
"Khan Zaman is ill, can you come?"

As we drive up the famous Grand Trunk Road from Gujranwala we recall this old friend's strange story. As a little Muslim
boy in a high village home in the Hazara Mountains he meets
a missionary family on holiday and cares for their baby son. He
returns to Chichawatni on the plains with them. In young manhood he becomes a Christian. There is much opposition in his village. His wife is embittered. He works for Mac and then for Mac
and Marie in Taxila Hospital. As his relatives become sick they
come to the hospital. He cares for them, returning good for evil.

His wife follows his faith, then a brother, then another brother and their families—more than thirty of his family and relatives over the years. Marie puts sparkling little daughter Zebunnissa into school, then college. She wants first to be a doctor then, if that is not possible, a teacher. God opens doors. Zeb goes to America, to Gordon Divinity School and returns to become Principal of Kinnaird High School in Lahore and an outstanding young churchwoman. Meanwhile, her father becomes cook to the missionary kids at their Murree Christian School.

When we arrive, late, he breaks into weeping for joy. "I was dead, now I am alive!" It is a violent quarrel between his children that distresses him so and has rocketed his chronic blood pressure.

He places the hands of Akram his son within my open hands and presses them shut. He takes the hands of Nirmala, Akram's wife, and places them similarly within Marie's hands. He presses them with his white bowed head. "Now Akram is *your* son and Nirmala is *your* daughter and I need fear for them no more." The errand is done and this loyal and beloved old man is at rest in his heart. It is all right now for us to go back home. He has transferred his charge.

We Start a Family

September 1957

We are naive, of course, to think that we can adopt a baby and be on our way back to Pakistan in two months. Bishop Chandu Ray suggests we start by contacting a friend of his in Croydon, south of London, in England. She is the adoption secretary for the Mission of Hope.

Miss Smith does not encourage us but will see us when we arrive. Marie by this time is forty-three years old, a little late for motherhood. However the past year at the Orphanage has given her plenty of experience and to me Marie is becoming younger, and lovelier, by the day.

Birdhurst Lodge in South Croydon is at that time a hostel for pregnant women to bear their children, a home for unmarried mothers and a refuge for single women in difficulty. It is also a children's home. Adoptions are arranged whenever the mothers seek that particular option.

Miss Smith talks to us carefully and her questions are searching. Her primary concern is the welfare of the child. We have no preference for a boy or a girl; we will take one of each if they are available. Marie is a nurse. Medical conditions in Pakistan are not adverse and Mission hospitals are within reach. The Sialkot Mission has many families with children. There is now a school for missionary children in Pakistan, it is no longer necessary for the children to go to India for schooling. We have had infant children in the Orphanage. Yes, we would prefer a baby rather than a child of some years.

Miss Smith seems encouraging; she is not negative about Marie's age or foreign nationality.

We talk about the limited time available to make arrangements. It is a little over one month. Our return journey on the Anchor Line *Cilicia* from Liverpool to Karachi is scheduled for November 7th. This is cutting it very fine. Discussions are currently taking place that will lead to legislation requiring a minimum period of six months in England before a child can be taken out of the country by adoptive parents. However we might be able to take a child with us on license and complete the adoption proceedings on our next furlough.

She will check into our references and let us know if a baby might be available. She will do her best.

On October 24th we receive a phone call. A baby, a boy, has become available, are we still interested? Are we! While we are waiting for Miss Smith to complete a prior interview Marie and I are shown around the new babies ward by the duty nurse. Among all the cots we both know *our* baby at once without being told. He is a long skinny streak of vigorous little humanity obviously prepared to take on and fight the whole world. His arms are flailing and his feet are kicking. The nurse sighs, "He just *hates* his orange juice."

Miss Smith points out that until the adoption processes are completed through the courts the parents, either of them, can request and will be given custody of the child. Is that a risk we are prepared to accept? It is. We expect to return to England in four years time and will anticipate completing the adoption processes at that time.

She has a baby boy whose mother has decided to put him forward for adoption. She tells us what she knows of both father and mother. As far as can be traced there are no latent health problems. He is seven weeks old. Would we like to see him? She leads us to little Master Orange Juice. This is the one. If we agree, we should come in on the 27th and be prepared to go with her to the Courts if necessary to complete the license. If everything goes well, we can take the child home with us that same day.

Our prayers are now focused. We will call the baby Timothy. (The missionary children to whom I have told stories of a little man half-a-thumb high called Timothy are certain that he has been named after a fairy.)

From that day until Marie's death forty years later she never failed to pray daily for that little child growing through boyhood and into manhood. When sent away to boarding school in the mountains at the age of six she wrote separate letters each day without fail to him and to his *almost a twin* brother. She never failed to hope and expect the best from him and she was rarely disappointed. He was everything we hoped for and we were so right for each other.

It is not only our prayers that are focused. So are our activities. Suddenly we have to equip ourselves in a few short days with four years supplies for a child, buy a huge stock of diapers and feeding bottles, a buggy with a carry-cot (that invaluable possession goes on down the line to other missionary families) and hosts of other things that my mother, veteran of ten children herself, advises as necessary. Terylene netting against flies and mosquitoes, toys for various ages and a range of clothing. My brothers and sisters, enjoying our confusion, contribute from their own experience and supplies. I notify the shipping company that there will be another passenger for their passenger list.

My father, somewhat jaded with the experience of a clamorous family, wonders if we know what we are letting ourselves in for.

On the ship at Liverpool are Charlie and Beatrice Chirnside, our future neighbors at Daska while we are at Hajipura fifteen miles away. They have with them a little boy, David, born less than three weeks before Tim. They will become close friends as the years pass.

At the Karachi orphanage our children, Lily, Barbara, Akhtar and Shamim, Parveen and Hussaina, Robbina and the others gather around the buggy and wonder where the baby has come from and whether the baby will grow up able to speak Punjabi and Urdu as they do.

Lilian

September 1956 - September 1957

There are two Lilians in our orphanage family. One is a little roly-poly two-year old who comes to us not long after we settled in. The pitiful little child is terrified, she is inconsolable and just turns her face into her bedding and cries and cries. She won't touch food, she just cries. I don't recall her family background nor do I recall any relatives coming to inquire about her. She doesn't speak our language. The other children of her age try to share their happiness with her but to no avail. Jhaggoo and Janebai try to cuddle her but she will have none of it. A doll is placed on her cot beside her but it means nothing to her. Marie sits down beside her and just talks gentle things to her, Lily cries all the more.

Several days after her arrival Marie is rejoicing when I come home from work. When the little child thinks she is alone she reaches out and touches the doll. Nothing happens. She touches a hand. Nothing happens. Then a leg. Still nothing happens. She pulls the doll's dress. The doll comes toward her. She touches its hair. She likes the feel of it. She smiles. She begins to touch it all over. Marie reaches over and covers the doll with an edge of Lily's blanket. Lily pulls it off. Marie puts it back on again. Lily pulls it off again, looks up at Marie and bursts out laughing. Marie laughs with her and covers the doll once more and brings something to eat. Lily eats. We walk over together to see this little transformation.

There is a poem of Leigh Hunt's that I've altered just a little:

Lily hugged me when we met.
Jumping from the cot she lay in,
Time, you thief, who love to put
Fruits in your list, put that in,
Say I'm weary; say I'm sad,
Say that health and wealth have missed me
Say I'm growing old but add
Lily hugged me.

No child's eyes sparkle like Lily's. No child has a greater sense of fun. No child lives more fully every minute of her day than Lily. No child is more determined to perch herself on Poppa's lap than Lily. She is pure, pure joy. The whole world is hers. Fifty years have passed. Lily will be a grandmother somewhere. Do her eyes still sparkle so? I do not know although I dare to hope. In my heart though she is enshrined with so many lovely others who like Peter Pan will never grow up. They are there like draughts from a spring to refresh with their laughter a tired old Englishman now far away from remembered places.

There is however another Lilian, very different, who also becomes Marie's and my daughter while we are at the orphanage.

There are four well renowned schools in Murree. The elevation among the mountains to the north of the Punjab, about 6,500 feet above sea level, means relatively cool summers and snow in winter. St. Lawrence's school is a boarding school for boys, the Jesus and Mary Convent School, run by nuns, is a school for girls and for younger boys. Murree Christian School, based in a disused garrison church on the outskirts, caters largely for missionary and non-Pakistani children. St. Denys School for girls is, or was, run by Englishwomen from a lay order of High Anglicans.

We've not been long at the orphanage when, one day early in September, Marie receives a telegram. Telegrams are the usual form of urgent communication since the nation's telephone system is in its very early unreliable stage.

MURREE MARIE OLD REQUEST INTER-
CEPT TWO GIRLS LEFT RAWALPINDI
FOR KARACHI BY TRAIN STALLARD

It is not difficult to fathom out what this means. Miss Stallard is the stalwart woman principal of St. Denys School. Obviously two of her girls have absconded by train to Karachi and she wants them intercepted.

Marie wastes no time. The telegram is dated yesterday. The girls will presumably be heading for the terminus, Karachi City Station. Possibly someone might be waiting to meet them there. However there is an earlier halt a couple of miles before the terminus, which allows passengers for the cantonment and the hajji camp for pilgrims to alight. Marie heads there in time to meet the first train arriving from Rawalpindi, a thousand miles up-line.

She's in luck; well maybe it isn't luck. She walks quickly through the train pushing her way past porters and passengers who are crowding the aisles. She does not know who she is looking for or what they look like. The train is packed with passengers standing in the aisles, grabbing luggage. Time is flying; she is not going to get through the train before it pulls out.

She is not yet halfway through the train, passengers are clearing and then there, on a bench seat facing her, she spots two girls, both about eighteen years old. One is a white girl and the other, a brunette, has an olive complexion, possibly a very light Pakistani complexion or perhaps Anglo-Indian. They look away from her, out of the window as soon as they see her but it is too late.

"Are you girls from St. Denys?" They nod dumbly, instinctively, shocked to have been intercepted before the Karachi City terminus. "I have been sent to meet you and take you home. Come quickly, here give me some of your luggage." Marie takes one of the cases from the rack. The two girls respond without question to undoubted authority, grab other pieces of luggage and scramble after her. Marie stands at the door to the railway carriage to block any attempt by the guard to send the train on its way before her charges are extricated.

By the time I arrive home from work to discover our family has swollen by two, Marie has sent a telegram to Miss Stallard and has unearthed the girls' story. Jean is the daughter of a British diplomat. Lilian is from a Lahore family, a railway family. The girls have met two Royal Air Force boys who are on holiday in Murree from the airbase at Mauripur that is having its runway extended. They have sneaked out from school at night to meet. They aren't quite sure they have fallen in love but they like the romantic thoughts. They are unhappy and bored at St. Denys. The young men have promised to help them if they can get themselves down to Karachi and have been waiting at Karachi City station. All their plans have been going well until the Cantonment Station.

The girls are settled in a room upstairs near ours, they have washed the dust of the journey away and Marie is serving tea as though this is a day of undisturbed routine and they are longtime residents.

Jean is sure that before long one of her parents will be down to pick her up and take her home. With Lilian the situation is different. She pleads with us. She doesn't want to go back to the school and she doesn't want to go back to her family in Lahore. Can't she stay with us, please? At least for a little while.

Stuart, our best man at our wedding, is staying with us. Obviously these RAF men need to be informed and, Stuart surmises, they need to learn a few lessons about behavior with girls. Armed with the men's names he drives out to see the British officer in charge of the RAF detachment. He returns several hours later well satisfied his errand has been dealt with.

Lilian proves to be a lovely girl. She is a daughter to us for a year. She is pretty and vivacious. She keeps herself neat and trim. She loves the security at the orphanage and at the same time she enjoys the increasing freedom we allow her as we come to know her. We trust her and she gives little reason for us to doubt that trust. Jean has been collected by her grateful parent within a day or so but there are no contacts from Lilian's family except for exchanged letters.

Lilian wishes to study a secretarial course. There is an evening course available not far from Elphinstone Street to which she can walk. However an unaccompanied young woman walking home each evening up the busy shopping street invites attention, especially when she is very pretty. Lilian tells me she is being followed by a stranger when she leaves school each night. I arrange with her that at 8 o'clock one particular evening I will be standing outside Bliss the Chemists. If the young man is following her she is to nod her head in his direction and continue straight on home.

I surprise myself with my own vehemence. I swing the young man round as though he has been hit in the shoulder by an artillery shell and ram my face within an inch of his. I have observed that any limitations in expression in Urdu due to my complete failure to understand simple grammatical rules, genders and tenses disappear in certain situations where clarity and emphasis is called for. I become for a few transient moments a Pauline ora-

tor endued with Churchillian vocabulary. Does he not understand
he has been following *my* daughter? *My* daughter! I shake him like
a rag doll. Does he not know that following *my* daughter is virtually a *capital* offense in Pakistan? Has he ever experienced police
flogging or matches under the fingernails! Every time he opens
his mouth to say anything I bellow more words, a torrent, into it
as though it is a third ear. The crowd of shoppers has formed an
amazed circle around this foreigner spewing forth such language.
I include them in so that they also are his accusers. What would
they do if this *wretch* followed *their* daughter!

I give him a final warning of what will happen to him if I ever
see him again, shake him violently and he runs away full speed in
the direction from which he has come.

Lilian never sees him again, nor do I.

One day Lilian asks me if it is possible to be a Catholic and
still remain a Christian. I describe as best and as fairly as I can the
differences between Catholic and Protestant belief.

Lilian has met a young Italian, Giuliano, he and his father are
running an engineering company of some sort, and she wants us
to meet him. Can he come around to the Orphanage and visit her
so that we might have an opportunity to meet him.

Giuliano comes one evening. He behaves very properly. He is
polite and deferential. Lilian and he sit and talk while Marie and
I busy ourselves at the other end of the large room. Most people
in Pakistan seem to know that Ken and Marie go to bed at nine
o'clock. Giuliano apparently is not aware of this.

At nine o'clock I show him to the gate and instruct the watch-
man that he is not to be allowed in again without my permission.
This is one of these rapacious young men taking, or trying to take,
advantage of susceptible young women. He isn't going to succeed
with Lilian.

A last cameo I have of Giuliano is our discussion through the bars of the bolted gate.

"You love her! I have heard that story before. You are like all the rest. The girl is naive and defenseless and you are out to exploit her. Go away and don't come back, don't ever come back!"

I have a recent letter from Lilian, from Italy. She is full of appreciation for Marie and for the goodness she met with.

> *Dear Poppa,*
> *If I had not left St. Denys that year I never would have met you both. One silly action led to a very positive thing for me. I have not been back to Pakistan since we left in 1962. My sons are grown up and married and we have a lovely grandson who is now eleven. Giuliano and I have been married for forty years now.*

Lilian never did become a Roman Catholic and is still an Anglican. She is also still very much our daughter.

More Sisters for Tim

Let me tell you about several more daughters we acquire along the Way. The adoption process is not limited in its impact to the new parents and the child adopted. There can be a wonderful extended richness in the intermingling of families if governed by love and goodwill and understanding.

One day, after Marie has returned to join me in Gujranwala in the late seventies, we have a letter from Tim in England. Would we mind if he tries to find out who he is? He doesn't want to hurt us but he would like to know who he really is. We encourage him to pursue his inquiries although he must be prepared to be hurt. The event that has brought us together has happened more than twenty years ago and the lives of his natural parents have moved on. He might well have been deliberately forgotten as an unwanted *blip* in their memories.

We have known however, and Tim also knew, that before the adoption formalities were completed his father has gone to Birdhurst Lodge. His circumstances have changed and he now wants to take his child back. He has married and has shared the secret of his son with his wife. Although initially reluctant, she agrees Jose should attempt to get the child into his custody and their care. He goes to Croydon but eventually decides to leave the child where he is on the recommendation of Miss Smith.

This is not known to us in Pakistan. Only when, on our next

furlough, we are arranging for Colin's adoption, does Miss Smith tell us that Tim's natural father has reluctantly been persuaded to leave the child in our hands.

So the years pass.

Jose and Violante have an only daughter, Susan. They dote upon her. They are able, with a generous employer's help, to give Susan an excellent education. She is in every way a credit to them.

One day her father phones his wife from London. He needs a certain paper urgently. It is among his private papers upstairs. Will she please locate it and send it to him? Violante asks Susan to get it for her. Susan, a curious fifteen-year-old, is eager to explore the contents within a secret compartment of an antique secretary desk. She finds an envelope and in it a picture of a newborn baby and, obviously, its mother. The writing in the letter is unfamiliar. It bears a date before she was born. She asks her mother and is *loaded for bear* when eventually her father returns home.

What is this all about? Doesn't he know that all her life she has wanted a brother, needed a brother? Why hasn't he told her? Doesn't he love his daughter enough to share this wonderful news with her! What has he done about making contact? Has he met him? What does he look like? Does he look like him—or her? Who is the boy's mother? It obviously isn't her mother.

The questions are endless. Jose is full of sorrow he has made his daughter so angry. He gives her the photograph and the letter. She may do with them as she will.

Susan spends the next four years attempting to find her lost brother. It is one dead end after another.

After she finishes her schooling with a year abroad, she has majored in languages and is interested in furthering her career; she takes a job as a translator in Germany. Susan takes the traces of an unknown brother back with her to Germany.

Tim's inquiries bear fruit.

He discovers his father is Portuguese and, from the phone book, that he now lives in Eastbourne. His own birth name is Jose and he has been named after his father. At this time he is living only 25 miles away from the seaside town. Several times he drives down to Eastbourne and goes past the address. Occasionally he parks nearby and just looks at the house. Occasionally he sees people entering and leaving. Finally, just before Tim and his family depart for the United States with Youth With A Mission, he makes a positive move to contact his father. He has a close friend, also an adoptee with a similar history; phone the house in Eastbourne to see whether the father is at all interested in his son of long ago. The woman who answers the call explains the family is away in Portugal. However she, to Tim's great surprise, is aware of his existence and takes down the phone message and the contact details. She is able to send Tim his first pictures of his natural father. He hears nothing further before he leaves but what he has done proves, after a long delay, to be enough.

Maggie has sent the details of his phone call to Susan.

In Pakistan we receive a letter from Tim. He has heard from a girl called Susan who lives near Frankfurt. She says she is his sister. She invites him to come and see her. What do we think he should do?

His visit to Germany is a change point for both of them. Susan is delighted to have a brother at last. There are strange similarities between themselves. They share their experiences. Susan is being courted by a young American helicopter pilot. He also is called Tim. Susan is Catholic and her faith is important to her. Her new brother hears the story of her life in England, which could so easily have been his own. There is a gulf between them; Pakistan is very much a part of who he is!

Later Tim gets another urgent letter from Susan. Her father, their father, has had a serious car accident in Portugal and wants to see his son. Can the young Jose (Tim) come? If he will take a flight to Lisbon his father will meet him at the airport and they will go together to the village in Portugal where the family resides. Susan arrives the following day. For a short while Tim lives among and is a well-accepted part of a large Portuguese family that makes the Catholic faith an important feature of its common life.

Susan marries her young American swain and they return to the United States. When, on furlough, we visit Tim and Cathy who are working in Powhatan, Virginia, the young couple drive up to see us from Norfolk. Since Colin is Tim's brother then Colin must be her brother too. Furthermore if we are Tim's parents and she is Tim's sister then it follows as the night follows day that we are her parents also.

And so it has proved. We become friends not only to Susan but with her parents as well. Susan comes for Marie's funeral and helps with the arrangements. When Jose dies in Eastbourne and is buried from the Catholic Church there Susan asks that I read two of the lessons during the service. After all, we are family.

Kate is a newer daughter to us than Susan, although older in years. Tim, within the last couple of years or so, gains additional information about his mother that compares with the sparse information he already has about her. Her surname is the same and the address almost tallies. He receives a surprise phone call from Lynchburg, Kentucky, from Vivienne who thinks she is his half-sister on his mother's side. She shares family news. She has a sister Kate, still in England, they both know about him. They have tried, and failed, to find their younger sibling for many years. They have discovered his surname and once they had thought they had identified him. They are glad that person was not the right one.

Patty and I visit her sister, who happens to live on the outskirts of a village south of Reading in Berkshire in England. Kate is a farmer's wife, happily married to David. She is about fifty years old and has two children. She is delighted to see us and to hear about her half-brother. She had been about seven when Tim was born and with her sister Vivienne was living with her grandmother. She does not have happy recollections of her childhood and both girls left home as soon as possible.

When Tim visits us in 2004, David brings both Kate and Vivienne to see for the first time their half-brother. They regard each other curiously, trying to discern how their relationship betrays itself in mannerisms and characteristics. Kate responds warmly to Patty's genuine affection and concern for a new member of her family. She is herself delighted to acquire at last a father whom she can love.

She regularly phones Patty for a chat and to inquire how her Dad is.

Having an expanding family is great joy. It's the way He works, scattering largesse.

A Missionary—who, ME?

June 1957

Of the missionaries we know most closely, only Norval Christy is Presbyterian by background yet each of them spend their lives as members of a small Presbyterian mission. How does this come about?

Dorothy, Norval's wife, is a Baptist by religious development and is challenged to consider missions overseas as a vocation. It is a natural progression to concur with her husband's calling and for her, eventually, to take membership in the Presbyterian Church in the States.

In 1949 Mac brings back to Pakistan Marie, his wife, who is from the old Swedish Covenant, now Evangelical Covenant Church. Marie abhors religious categories among Christians but would have been termed a conservative evangelical. In the fall of 1948, shortly after her marriage, the Board of Foreign Missions of the United Presbyterian Church of North America (UPCNA) appoints her as an associate similarly to Mac. Their salary, deriving largely if not solely from Mac's home church in Hawthorne, they receive through the Board's field treasurer.

In 1955 I enter the picture. I have no particular desire to be a missionary (and no particular objection to it either). When, in September, during a visit to Taxila, I ask Marie to marry me I visualize we will complete my present contract, return to England and wait for God to show us both the next step forward. I do not know where or what that will be, I have no preferences, but God is capable of fulfilling His purposes for and in both our lives. All we have to do is to let Him do it.

I have promised that He could have the rest of my life. That is as far as it goes or needs to go.

Lock't in the congruence
Of God's purpose
There is a moment,
Elemental, solitary,
And strangely divine,
Diff'rent for each of us,
When time shall stop
And all His glory shine.
Time with its song of life
And all its darkness

> *Will then resume*
> *And others never know*
> *What has occurred*
> *While we are left*
> *Trying to understand*
> *What happened.*

It will be up to Him to reveal His Will in due course. His timing will be perfect; it always is perfect. It has to be because He exists outside of and beyond time and can see the end as well as the beginning.

Fifteen years previously in Plymouth God had told me that He had a purpose for my life. Had I chosen to examine that more closely I might have concluded that Pakistan is indeed a possible location. Moreover, to work amongst boys could conceivably involve me in being a missionary of some sort.

However I have not been thinking along those lines at all. I merely seek to be sensitive and responsive in a positive way to any divine leading I might receive. Marie is later to laugh over this approach. She, in agreeing to marry me, has had no intention of leaving Pakistan or, indeed, of breaking for more than a short while her relationship with the Sialkot Mission. It does not even occur to her that marrying me could conceivably take her away from Pakistan forever. Somewhat strangely we do not discuss in depth the variant views of our future. As events turn out she proves entirely right to be utterly relaxed within the unknown Will of God.

Two of the outstanding missionaries we have encountered are Dr. Orval Hamm and his wife, Lucy. Just as Norval and Dorothy give their lives to Taxila Hospital so, almost two hundred miles to the southeast Orval and Lucy, after a term in Egypt, give their lives to Sialkot Hospital. They are from Kansas and confirm to me that some of the best missionaries are farm boys and girls from the mid-west plains of America. Theirs is a very different kind of hospital. It has a nursing school, a busy obstetrics and gynecology unit and a lot of babies unwanted by their parents. It is located in a Punjabi city rather than in a village.

Orval and Lucy have been expecting Marie to come down from Taxila as matron of nurses. To their surprise she arrives with a young English civil engineer in tow as an escort. On the journey down they become engaged to be married in a little more than three months. If they are disappointed at the prospect of losing their nurse so soon they do not show it. They take the stranger in and respond valiantly to the observed need for some courting time and space. They find urgent cause most evenings to be over at the nurses' bungalow next door leaving their own drawing room available for their guest and any visitor he might have.

In gratitude and appreciating the situation that will be left at the hospital by my stealing their nurse I offer to Orval that when my engineering contract ends and before we return to England, possibly for good, I will convert a disused TB ward into a children's ward at the hospital for him. It should only take three or four months. He accepts this offer with alacrity.

Almost two years later the personnel committee of the Sialkot Mission meets.

They have had news from us that we expect to leave the orphanage in early September, will try to adopt a child in England and will be on our way back to Sialkot by early November. We are naive about how long it takes in a Western society to find and adopt a child. Permission to take it out of the country requires even longer. In our case, under a holy timetable, it took only as long as the time we had available.

The committee will need to make some financial arrangements for us while we are converting the ward. Without asking us about how long we might anticipate the job will take we are appointed as a short-term missionary couple in June of 1957 for a term of three years. So far no one has checked on my theology, my psychology, my religious suitability or whether I have even attended Bible School (I haven't). Four years later someone in the head office in the States, so we are told, realizes that our appointment has expired, there are no available further short term renewals but there is one slot available for a couple to serve in the Sialkot Mission on a lifetime appointment. This is where we are put.

Pause and recognize for a moment the complete short-circuiting of the careful and painstaking process by which missions must apply every possible precaution to the selection of missionary candidates. Had that short circuit not happened I can conceive no credible way that I could ever have been appointed as a missionary of the Sialkot Mission. I have never been to the United States. Theologically I am a macro-unknown. I have never been in any kind of Presbyterian Church outside Pakistan, I don't know what Presbyterians stand for and certainly I would have failed any kind of normal selection process.

Yet here we are, appointed for life and, although it still lies many years away, heading unerringly towards Gujranwala and Boys' Town in the Punjab to fulfill God's purposes for our lives.

The Sialkot Mission

November 1957

Shakespeare's Henry V before Agincourt rejects the desire expressed to him by his compatriots for more alongside them to help them fight the French.

> *. . . if we are marked to die we are enow*
> *To do our country loss; and if to live,*
> *the fewer men the greater share of honour.*

> *He which hath no stomach for the fight, let him depart.*
> *We few, we happy few, we band of brothers;*
> *For he today that sheds his blood with me*
> *Shall be my brother.*

Twice in my life I have been privileged to be part of a unity far greater than myself and been proud to be but a minor part of a great enterprise.

The first is shared by all in Britain who know the exultation and pride and companionship in standing threatened and in company outnumbered after Dunkirk while the battle raged in the skies and on the seas.

The second is to be a member of a remarkable band of brothers and sisters graced by the name The Sialkot Mission.

Missionaries are not necessarily saints, they are just practicing Christians, flawed people, with a high religious calling but these are the nearest to a body of saints I shall ever encounter. I come from a very close family of brothers and sisters. I never expect to find its like, or even better, in a group of people brought together by apparent chance. I come into the Sialkot Mission indirectly, through a side door, by marriage to someone who has also come in through a side door, by marriage to someone who had chosen association with it.

I come into it at a time when there are many in the Mission who have first come out to India in the twenties and others, younger and more spry, in the thirties. They are wise and resilient and tested people. They have come for life and retirement is rushing too soon upon them. They are godly and temperate and filled with practical commonsense. They know the language of the land, often as well as their own native tongue. To some, second or third generation, it *is* their native language. They know the land and they know its people. They know their strengths and appreciate them. They know their weaknesses and seeing past them, love despite them.

The Mission's principles are tested by the fires of experience and the standards of Scripture. Wisely the Mission is run by the field missionaries and not from a head office bureaucracy. They have to live with the consequences of the actions they take so they think carefully before they act; they know only too well the people involved. Their principles are applied firmly but pragmatically.

They are Presbyterians, this band of brothers and sisters, strong on accountability and parliamentary procedures and Robert's Rules of Order. The October Annual Meeting at the Christian Training Institute in Sialkot is always liable to have its hot debate interrupted by the appointed Parliamentarian drawing attention to a deviance or interpretation of the correct order of events and motions.

In the early Fifties there are slightly less than a hundred members of the Sialkot Mission. Perhaps as many as twenty might have been on furlough at any one time. Almost all are American, although, occasionally there will be a man or woman of Scots or English origin. There are always more women than men and thus specialties involving the nurture and teaching of women and girls and meeting their various needs flourish particularly well.

A typical Mission Station without an attached boarding school will involve two residences, stores for tents and equipment and quarters for servants and staff. One of the residences is occupied by a district missionary couple and the other residence by one or two unmarried women missionaries. Right after Annual Meeting, after any re-locations of missionaries have been made (usually after hot debate), preparations for winter touring in the districts will be hurried forward to get in a good session before Christmas.

One of the great strengths of the Sialkot Mission has been the readiness of its missionaries to leave their homes whenever it is not too hot and travel around their districts wherever there are responsive groups to be found. They will set up their tents for a week or two on the edge of a village, perhaps near the cemetery and near a well. If necessary they will bore a tube well for a hand pump.

The great capacities and skills of leadership of missionary women, often working in stations where there are no missionary men, are convincing proof, if such is needed, that God richly blesses women in Christian leadership who are called according to His Purpose.

The Mission runs, with very limited financial resources but with great management skills and initiatives, a vast enterprise of medicine and education. This includes dispensaries and hospitals, primary and boarding schools and a college. All the while it is helping a small and weak indigenous church to find its feet and develop its own leadership out of origins far distant and different from that of the mission.

Among many exceptional people in the early years of the Sialkot Mission there are perhaps two that can be noted, Andrew Gordon and James Barr.

James Barr and his wife establish the Gujranwala Mission Station in Khokherke and the Barr Training Institute of the Society for Community Development is named after him.

After thirty-two years service with the Sialkot Mission that he founded in 1855 Andrew Gordon summarizes his experiences so far.

"We consider," he writes, "the number of converts and their rapid growth, the thirty-five communicants of the first ten years increasing to seventy in the next six years; then this number rising to one hundred and fifty, or more than double, in the next four years; this again to six hundred in the following three years and finally becoming more than two thousand in the last three years." Almost all these converts have come not out of Islam or Sikhism but from the lower outcaste strata of Hinduism.

The great Mass Movement is yet to come in the first decade of the twentieth century. That will see immense church growth and the establishment of the Sialkot Convention. In those first patient years around the time of the Indian Mutiny and its horrors Andrew Gordon and his wife Rebecca seem forgotten by the church that has sent them. They lose their infant son to fever and see an average of seven converts each two years. Yet they keep on going! In our six characteristics for missionaries to be successful Marie and I listed tenacity as the final one. We who come later have great exemplars.

The End of an Era

Not with a bang but a whimper
November 1960

In November of 1960 we have completed the three years of our appointment with the Sialkot Mission.

Its home church, the United Presbyterian Church of North America, has entered into a merger with a much larger church, the Presbyterian Church, U.S.A. This will lead to a different way of doing Mission, conceived as *Mission on Six Continents*. Now Mission is to become *Relationships* and the struggling Synod of the Punjab is to become, ready or not, a *partner* with the PCUSA in a joint enterprise.

It can hardly be called an unqualified success. Churches stand between heaven and an indigenous culture and are drawn culture-wards. Missionaries who have spent their lives guiding the development step by step of national Christians towards maturity have found there are two, sometimes three, steps backward for every two steps forward. Rarely is there only one step backward and thus progress forward.

They know each national leader, pastor, layman and laywoman, from childhood. They know each knot in the tangled web of marriage affiliations. They recognize the power of the family unit as virtually unchallengeable and inexorable. They know and understand that the intimacies of family relationships not only guide but govern decisions.

They recognize the need for time, even time for generations to pass, so that the basic Christian ethics of social behavior can become understood and receive unselfish response. They recognize how individually they themselves have benefited from centuries of cultural inheritance within a framework of first Catholic and then Protestant teaching and example. The necessity for truth and honesty and integrity in all aspects of personal behavior is ingrained within them. They are themselves prepared to sacrifice pragmatic advantage for principle and rejoice to see such hoped for but unexpected signs in others. It is necessarily a long slow journey.

They have an immense influence, these missionary elders. They are beloved in a way we younger ones can never hope to be loved. Seeking to understand the qualities that make certain missionaries outstanding in their influence I ask a number of leading Punjabi Christians about the missionary they admire most and why. I of course have my lineup of the *greats* already on their pedestals but I want confirmation from the other side of the street.

Their answers surprise me. Occasionally there is concurrence with my own opinion but always for a different reason. Without exception the missionary they admire most is not chosen for exceptional effectiveness or mighty works, for powerful preaching or ardent praying, for leadership or charisma or vision but always because he or she has tapped my respondent on the shoulder and sent him or her to school or to college or to seminary or has suggested a personal vocation and helped make it possible.

The church of the Punjab needs that influence between individuals to continue but it is unable to express itself adequately. In the States it is not even recognized as an asset but discarded as paternalism.

The situation is similar to what the British Government itself faced in India. Wavell, the Viceroy, understood only too well and concurred in, the aspirations of the Indian peoples. But it would take time, a decade, maybe even two decades, to turn over to the claimant disputive aspirants for power an India that would not lapse into chaos. The real power lay not with the British Government but with the constituency at home behind it. That was where ultimately decisions made would be tested for acceptability. Wavell was backed by the counsel of that superb cadre of public servants, the Indian Civil Service. They knew the people. They lived in the civil divisions and districts throughout that vast country. If order was to be preserved and the hand-over not result in an uncontrollable outpouring of racial and religious hatred time was needed to select, induct and then assist the new leadership. The answer, if indeed answer it was, was to replace Wavell with Mountbatten.

So with the Sialkot Mission. It has apparently served its purpose and now there is no longer need for it. It will wither on the vine even if it does not die outright. It might continue to exist as a legal entity but from now forward the Commission on Ecumenical Mission and Relations of the Presbyterian Church U.S.A., drawing upon all the wisdom at home, will be making the decisions that matter.

In May, 1961 Marie, Timmy and I head off to Karachi for a sea journey to England and beyond. Marie will be going home to the States after eight years; it will be her menfolk's first journey there. We will be coming back. That is taken for granted. There is much building work unfinished and the Fosters will not leave the Christian Training Institute in Sialkot until we have returned.

Wah Church and Wah Cottage

December 1958 – March 1960

Although I have built a mosque at the cement factory in Hyderabad I have not previously built a church. It is appropriate that the first church I build will be a Memorial Church for Mac.

Uncle Willie Sutherland and, I am sure, the Hawthorne Gospel Church in New Jersey, Mac's home church, have raised the funds. It looks as though there will be enough to start and complete a small memorial church seating two hundred in the cantonment of the gigantic ordnance factory at Wah. This is the location of the work, evangelism and literacy, that Mac and Marie had been so involved in before his death. The local congregation has also been raising funds for six years.

Uncle Willie has obtained from the government a good and level site for a church not far from the Great Mosque. The Catholic father also has a site on the Grand Trunk Road and during the concurrent construction of his building I am able to act as a technical resource to him.

We have come down from Murree when snow makes it impossible to continue building houses. We return to the plains delighted with permission from the mission to rent accommodation away from the hospital on the other side of Wah Cantonment in Wah village. We are aware that a beautiful and isolated little cottage was empty. Mahmud Hayat Khan agrees to rent the property to us. Two young missionary teachers from Murree Christian School are to be our primary guests during the two winters we are there.

In the three months before returning to the Murree hills in the spring, however, it is only possible to get an eye ward started at the Mission hospital several miles from Wah.

During the summer while I am completing the houses at Sandes Home in Murree, Marie takes on a spell of language supervision of new missionaries learning Urdu at the Language School.

By August we are again in Wah Springs. This is a time of great personal happiness. Our little boy is a toddler, just two. We, like most parents with a first child, are fascinated with everything he does. Marie walks him daily in his buggy down to the old Moghal gardens of which she has earlier and precious private memories. She meets and makes friends with members of the Wah Family as well as the ordinary passers-by and promenades her frequent guests through the lovely formal gardens.

I am initially busy at home designing the church, a reinforced concrete portal framed building with precast concrete roofing and a bell tower. It will have a ship's bell fetched up from Karachi. I am not an architect but I am learning fast that the Mission builder needs to apply his hands to whatever has to be done. I am also taking a Sunday evening service in English and a weekly Bible class for the British folks in the factory.

Marie resumes her interest with the women's work and literacy in the cantonment. While she is away she can leave her son without concern with Khan Zaman's family.

From across the Grand Trunk Road, at Aram, Farrukh becomes a frequent visitor, especially at teatime. Farrukh has been to the Jesus and Mary convent school in Murree but confesses his inability to appreciate the Christian teaching of *turning the other cheek*. "When someone does me wrong" he asserted grimly, "I hit them back and I hit them so hard they stay down for a *very* long time. Your teaching is an invitation to assault! It's quite incomprehensible." His parents, courteous and friendly, frequently invite us to Aram to meet eminent guests that might be visiting them from overseas.

We have two guest rooms. There are frequent guests; usually, but not always, missionaries. Up above the house, now known as Wah Cottage, on the other side of the road leading to the village, live Khan Zaman and his family. It is there Timmy's Punjabi is being honed. That is his first language, Urdu is his second and English his third. He spends every spare moment there being a Punjabi child, the youngest child in a family of many children. Not all the words he picks up there are known to us nor are they all suitable to tea-table conversation. His bedtime stories feature water buffaloes, camels, bullock carts, steam rollers and tar boilers.

At the end of October we have the groundbreaking ceremony for the church. Many Pakistanis and English people are present. Now work gets under way on the church proper. A garage and incomplete pastor's house has already been built. Services are being held in the garage. I take Timmy the four miles from home on the crossbar of my bicycle. The masons give him a trowel and turn him loose to play with the mortar and bricks in the foundations until it is time to return home.

I have by this time acquired new from England a wonderful small green Winget concrete mixer, a 7/5 that is my joy and pride. For more than thirty years that machine, belching ever greater clouds of black diesel smoke when starting, is as reliable as daybreak. When I retire it is still going strong!

Bricks, nails, screws and glass are all in short supply and difficult to find but throughout construction it is cement that will continue to be our primary shortage.

I estimate we will need nine hundred bags of cement. After seven months of almost weekly visits to the Rawalpindi offices of the cement company we begin work with only fifty bags of cement. By mid-November we have received and used a further two hundred bags. We count that a miracle. Now we are again almost out of cement.

A helpful friend, knowing our dilemma, arranges a truckload, two hundred bags, for us on the black-market. There will be no extra charge to pay; it is an act of kindness.

Now here is a dilemma. I struggle with the morality of the situation. We are desperate for cement. There are no bribes or additional charges. This opportunity might not recur. My labor force will perhaps need to be reduced if not completely dismissed. Yet this is not my work. It is God's work. He has taught me to trust Him and has never let me down. Is He not capable of providing *clean* cement for His own work? I decline the cement with thanks, feeling a fool to turn down such a generous offer at a time of such shortage. The difficulties continue; we manage to get four or five bags at a time and ration their use. Never once, though, are we ever completely out of cement.

After fifteen wonderful months at Wah Cottage we move back to Taxila Hospital. I do not recall the reason. The spring eye season is well under way and perhaps Marie's help is needed there. If a doctor has gone on furlough, a house at the hospital may have become temporarily available. Or Mahmud might need use of the cottage for some of the Wah Family. From now on we will always live on a Mission Compound in an institution with other missionaries but these too brief months on the edge of the village of Wah under the shadow of the Pir Baba Wala Hill are among the happiest we spend in Pakistan.

In the front of the church adjacent to the pulpit I prepare a large simple cross of polished shisham wood to act as a visual focus for the congregation. Before I can install it I find one morning in its planned place a large school clock and a proud pastor admiring its placement and checking its time. This is tricky. Obviously that is the wrong place for a clock but how to tactfully move it elsewhere?

"That's very nice, Padri sah'b, but I have prepared a cross, here it is, that I thought might look very well there."

Padri sah'b admires the cross. He agrees that the front wall is the right place for the cross. "Shall we put it above or below the clock?" he questions gently.

I have ordered for the front facade of the church twenty-four inch square panes of blue turquoise glass from Pilkingtons of St. Helen's in England. Every pane of the first shipment arrives broken. It is the same with the second shipment. The third shipment, allowing for spare sheets in an increased order, yields just enough to cover the area. Every sheet is precious. There are no spare sheets. I am fixing each sheet myself. Some of the sheets are sixteen feet above the floor. One morning I am fixing the last, highest sheet, reaching almost above my head on rickety scaffolding. The scaffolding tilts when the man steadying it moves away and I feel myself falling, falling backwards.

I lie for a while on the floor, on my back, still conscious, and conscious of great pain. I think that probably my back is broken. I do not try to move. Nur ul Haq finds some paper. I reach to a pocket for a pencil without moving myself and scribble a note to Dr. Brown at the hospital. I tell Nur ul Haq to take my bicycle and hurry. Someone covers me with a blanket. It seems hours. The workmen move quietly about their work around me.

Dr. Brown finds me gray and motionless but still conscious. He checks me with scrupulous care. There are no obvious signs of a break although clearly there is serious damage. He calls for the help of several of the men and moves me carefully to the car, the hospital has no ambulance, makes me comfortable and takes me slowly back to the hospital. Marie has had the news, a bed in the house is ready and after X-rays had been taken I am delivered into her care.

Several of the lower vertebrae of the sacroiliac have been chipped and severely compressed as I landed in virtually a sitting position on the concrete floor. Fortunately I have no head injuries of any consequence. Specialists recommend a spinal fusion but I choose to let things be. For many years thereafter I suffer persistent back pain. When that occurs I become irritable and bad tempered. Marie is always generously quick to inquire whether my back is hurting and usually one is associated with the other. The only other consequence, a minor one, is that I can no longer bear to drive a motorcycle.

At the end of September we move on to our next assignment down to Sialkot. Building jobs, particularly there, are piling up in the queue that is steadily getting longer. Long-term missionaries, the Fosters, are retiring from the Christian Training Institute and we are to use the Lal Kothi, the red house, as our next home.

Bob Noble, chaplain at Taxila in place of Mac and Uncle Willie, undertakes to complete the last details of the church. A school is operating in the three attached classrooms and the garage is still in use for the patient congregation seated on the ground. The pastor's house is virtually completed and in use. Early in December the McGuill Memorial Church is dedicated before a crowded congregation as the only Protestant place of worship in a city of fifty thousand people. The city has never stopped growing.

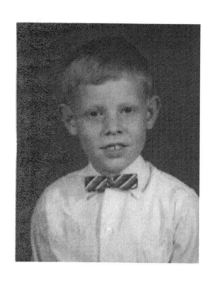

Colin

June 1961

From my first visit to the United States I gain an erroneous but absolutely favorable impression of the country and its people. I am like Khan Zaman in his judgments.

We have purchased a new Mini in England for a little over four hundred pounds and have picked it up from the docks in New York. The drive from the docks is terrifying but I gradually become accustomed to being a minnow among whales.

Our stay in New York at a church house enables us (or requires us) to visit the church headquarters on Riverside Drive. Timmy has previously been in a Punjabi school at Sialkot. When we put him into a nearby school where Spanish is the lingua franca, it tends to confuse him. He is only four and fortunately we are not too long there. We are able to visit Mac's family. Maynard loves the way this confused little blond boy pronounces *butter* with t's instead of d's.

We drive across the States, through Montana and on to Selah and Yakima in Washington. I find the average temperature inside the centrally heated homes stiflingly hot but the people are as warm-hearted as their indoor temperatures. Without exception they are friendly, open and helpful. They are mostly church related but not all of them. If there are any unpleasant Americans I do not meet them. Marie's relatives welcome us with open arms and there are many friends keen to meet Marie's English husband and son. There are excursions to remembered places in the high eastern Cascades that make me wonder how Marie could ever have left such natural beauty. I realize how much she misses these native surroundings and how in the torrid heat of our monsoon summers she longs for the mountains of home.

We join the Westminster Presbyterian Church in Yakima, feeling that although neither of us knows much about U.S. Presbyterianism we are representing that church in Pakistan. It proves a happy association.

Now it is time to return to Pakistan. Leaving the state of Washington, we take a southern route through Salt Lake City. Crossing the Rocky Mountains we drive over a pass in excess of 11,000 feet. It is a challenge for our tiny car, a Mini, but it just sails over with no problems.

When we reach the East coast, Mac's younger brother, Larry, takes the car from us the day we leave.

We have a date with a little boy in England and need to be

there early in November to be able to keep a deadline with our return by sea from Liverpool six months later.

Miss Smith, our friend at the Mission of Hope, has let us know that a little four-year-old boy will be available for us on our return from the States. She tells us all that she is able about the family and its circumstances.

Within a day or so of disembarking from the Queen Mary we are in Croydon. Timmy is already looking forward to his brother. I pop into my pocket a white Dinky toy, an ambulance, as we leave home. The little boy has a sister. We are anxious they not be separated and would have taken both children but the mother desires to keep her daughter.

His mother brings Colin. How hard it must be to say farewell forever to that little ginger haired boy that she has cared for so lovingly for four years. Her home circumstances just do not permit her to keep him. How hard too for the little boy who can never understand why his mother gave him away. We do not meet his mother although she is probably standing aside in some secluded place to see her son's new parents. Marie catches a glimpse of her bringing Colin, a lovely young woman, and treasures that glimpse.

We love him the moment we see him, little lost boy in a blue blazer and gray shorts. I put my arm around him and dig out the Dinky toy to play with on the table. We push it to and fro towards each other while Marie chats with Miss Smith and allows her new son to get accustomed to the people around him.

This little boy is different from Tim. He is accustomed to double-decker red buses and going upstairs to bed. He has prior memories whereas Tim has none and it is important that these memories be nurtured and treasured and not violated or dismissed.

We do not change his first name, he remains Colin, but his surname changes. He hardly notices that. He and his brother are getting used to each other. Timmy is finding two people have claims on the toys, not just himself. They quickly become friends, fast friends, and almost inseparable.

Colin is four months older than Timmy. I overhear in the co-op in Bromley a lady asking the two little dress-alikes whether they are twins. "Oh no, we're brothers" one replied.

"How old are you?" "Four." "And how old are you?" "Four," comes the other answer.

The British Adoption laws have changed. It is only possible to take children out of the country after six months residence. Only days before we sail back those six months are completed and then the full adoptions are processed.

There is one snag. Marie and I cannot prove we are married! Our marriage lines have been stolen with other things from our luggage and the marriage register in Taxila has been eaten by white ants! Only Miss Smith's affirmation that she has indeed seen our marriage certificate when we had first taken Timmy saves the day and we sail on May 12th, Colin's birthday, on schedule.

(Colin is now in Arkansas studying to be an accountant and a grade school teacher after more than a decade in the U.S. Airborne serving in the U.S. and Korea. His dearest treasure is a well-worn Dinky toy, an ambulance, with most of its white color now worn off.)

Missionary Kids

September 1963

Colin and Tim are six. Tim has already attended a Punjabi school in Hunterpura before Colin joins him. Then they both attend the Convent school in the Sialkot cantonment. Now they have reached the age for boarding school. They are about to complete the essential requirement for almost all children of missionaries. Going away to boarding school.

We put them on the train to Pindi at Wazirabad thirty miles away from our home. Their footlockers, distinctively colored for easy recognition, are full of the neatly ironed and sorted clothing they will be needing, snacks, toys and games and, tucked away somewhere for each of them, a teddy bear.

MK's form one of the greatest and richest fraternities in the world. They give a false picture of themselves. They seem perpetually to be struggling to counter and explain the agonies of reentry into their home cultures and the emotional pains and results of their isolations from parents during boarding school years. True that may be but it is only part of a much greater richer truth.

MK's are truly international people, equipped like few others for the interchanges that link the thoroughfares of the world. They have it over kids with parents in diplomatic, military or foreign service or in the overseas commercial world. Their roots are set strong into the lands where they live as children, they acquire naturally second, sometimes even third, languages without even trying.

Usually their parents remain in one land of service throughout their children's childhood. Through their homes pass as guests and visitors a continuous flow of exceptional and often exciting people. Many will be saints and some, if our house is a criterion, will be outstanding sinners. Most, but not all, of the parents have a deep and abiding, even compelling, love for the land in which they serve and for its people. When their children are grown they too become ready-made and fluent ambassadors for a land other than their own.

Many, though not all, develop close childhood friendships with national children that last throughout a lifetime. They are loved children at every stage. The MK schools, frequently set in gentler climates and higher altitudes than where their parents work, are staffed by teachers and boarding staff drawn by the same impulses and calls that their parents have.

They are not parked off out of the way by parents happy to see them go but are yielded up reluctantly to the constraints of circumstance and covered all the while they are apart by prayer.

Their parents have no ambition for themselves, save to be faithful, but much for their children. Because they are rarely at home other than on the long school closure they are not taken for granted while they are able to be there at home but every day becomes a special day. How quickly those calendar dates whirl round when the children are on holiday! The natural annual cycles of sowing and harvest become instead the journeys to and from school by plane or train, by bus or car, sometimes many hundreds of miles, occasionally across national frontiers.

They are encouraged and supported and challenged and stimulated by the adults around them. At a much earlier age than their cousins at home they develop independence, resilience, patience and initiative. They encounter radically different customs and culture and ways of thinking. They recognize early that most other people see things differently than the way they do. They adjust and learn tolerance rather than judgment. They become self reliant and self disciplined; a few even become tidy! None among the boys learn to change their underwear or socks without being reminded.

They are, or were, protected from the influences of television and electronic entertainment and learn to create their own music, dramas and activities. They are fanatically keen on the progress of their own school in sports and art over against other similar schools in neighboring countries.

I read somewhere that a greater proportion of MK's make the pages of Who's Who than any other group. I would expect that.

For most of ten years of their early life they are away from home in a small school of perhaps only one or two hundred pupils drawn from a dozen nationalities. Their warmest memories, their closest friendships, their most enduring relationships are those with their school friends.

Occasionally these relationships, some crossing international boundaries, mature into marriage. Sometimes too these childhood sweethearts come back to the land where they met each other and start over the next generation of missionary parents and their MK's.

From now on our lives as a family will be governed by schooling requirements. Except for one furlough period in the States during 1967 / 68 the boys have no other schooling except at Murree Christian School. The setting is an old British Army garrison church in Gharial just outside Murree. Until the boys leave and come to Britain in 1974 Marie will, apart from furloughs, spend each summer from May to September in the hills. She is making a home for the boys so that they can continue to attend school although the boarding hostel is closed for the summer. In winter the snows and cold weather cause closure early in December for three months. Those three months are the best time of the year for us parents on the plains and, frequently, for the children also.

Ken, Tim, Marie and Colin

War

September 1965

On September 6th Marie and the two boys and I are in Kabul. I have been consulting about the hospital building that is needed there with Seymour. Task settled, we go to the airport to fly back to Peshawar and are told to our complete surprise that the flights have been suspended because India and Pakistan are at war.

Attempts to gain information from the Pakistan Embassy are unsuccessful.

We decide to catch an early local bus the following day heading for Jalalabad and hopefully make it to Torkham, the Afghanistan / Pakistan border point at the western end of the Khyber pass, before dark.

It indeed is a local bus. We are the only Westerners on it and share it with black or gray-bearded, black-turbaned men and burqa clad women crowded onto every other seat except the ones occupied by a goat and some sheep.

The bus does not take the usual main road following the Kabul River valley and gorge but takes off south for the slow dirt roads of the high plateau where its stopping points seem to consist only of large mud-walled caravanserais every fifteen or so miles. This is obviously not the usual tourist route but we refresh ourselves at each sarai with tiny china cups of pale sweet tea (cava) from battered little teapots. Where we can, we buy the large misshapen unleavened bread to chew until the next stop.

Eventually, about midday, the bus descends into Sarobi where the Russians have been installing a hydroelectric scheme across the river to complement the road they have built from Kabul to the Khyber. Now travel is faster. Jalalabad, the nearest major town to the Khyber is left behind, the Afghan customs post eventually negotiated and we walk gratefully back to our home territory and greet our Pakistani border guards like long lost brothers. They too know little about how the war is going except that they know we are winning.

For a while we wait in Landikotal for the bus to leave, wandering through the little shops in the bazars that are rich with smuggled goods.

The bus ride through the Khyber Pass is in the gathering dusk. By the time we are through Jamrud it is dark. We go straight to the railway station in Peshawar. Everything is blacked out. When I strike a match to search in my briefcase for papers it provokes yells of anger. We catch a night train to Rawalpindi.

Reports there are that bombs have been dropped near Raja Bazar and we waste no time recovering the parked truck and heading up the hill to Murree.

Marie and the boys will remain there until things sort themselves out while I am heading back without delay to Sialkot to join Orval Hamm at the hospital. We have moved there from C.T.I. in April to continue with building work. Radio reports are talking of fighting around Sialkot, a major continuing tank battle near Chawinda five miles away to the east and stiff resistance by the Pakistan army. Rumors are that the city has been shelled and the hospital hit. There is no news as to casualties.

It is unlikely that we will be able to replenish fuel for the truck, so I leave that behind, but John Wilder is willing to divert to Sialkot and drop me off before heading for Lyallpur. That way he can get news from Orval and pass it on.

The road from Wazirabad to Sialkot is full of the tragic debris of war that has become so common on television screens. Refugees of all shapes, sizes and descriptions; the elderly carrying the frail and infirm. Horse taxis with so much load it is a wonder the hooves of the horse have any traction. Buses threading their way slowly through the hastening crowd with the roof racks as crowded with people as the inside. Always the incredible junk of valued possessions that it is essential to save. No, the Indians have not yet entered the city though there are reports they are across the Aik in several places so it will be any time now. We are, once we get through Sambrial and across the canals and approaching Ugoke, able to move at little more than walking pace. Troops are camped in the C.T.I. playing fields. The commanding general has taken over our old home, the Lal Kothi, for his headquarters but has sent assurances that the furnishings will be protected and returned.

Orval is glad to see us. Yes, a shell has landed just near the water tower, hitting the end of the babies' ward. Miraculously, although the children have been covered with debris, none is seriously hurt. Some, covered in red brick dust and yelling their heads off in terror, are still sitting on their potties as Orval and the nurses burst through the haze to recover them. Another shell has landed near the chapel but has done no damage. Generally the shells are going over the hospital and are being directed at the defenses rather than indiscriminately.

Since there is considerable anti-American feeling (not a deep rooted antipathy but you have to blame somebody) we agree that I will move around the town and represent the hospital to the authorities while Orval gets on with the medical concerns of the hospital. Among them is the care of the eighteen babies, the responsibility for the student nurses and the condition of Edward Balph, a wonderful old retired missionary builder who has come back out to help me and has been taken ill. Now is in his early eighties, he is bedridden and dying.

Two brief cameos of those days:

Most of the leaders of the Christian community have managed to get away from the city and its precincts. When news spreads around that the hospital is still functioning and that Orval and the two German nurses and I are also still around, we begin to get visitors, ordinary little people who feel abandoned and who know us. Many desperately need reassurance and they need help.

The people from Christiantown and C.T.I. come across to see me. We have lived among them for five years. Many are virtually penniless. Can I help them; can I lend them money to get to Jhelum or Martinpur? They will pay me back later. One basic principle for survival in an economy of the poor is that you never lend money. Loans are treated as a gift. If you can't afford to make a gift, then don't make the loan.

However these people are desperate and I know most of them. I take my building money, about three thousand rupees, and loan it out in dribs and drabs to the needy until it is all gone. I tell them that this isn't my personal money, if they don't repay me I will have to make the amount good myself but I will take that risk because of their need.

To my great amazement all of the money comes back after the cease-fire. It takes some time for them all to return—will the cease-fire hold?—but as they do they come over to see me and pay me back, each one of them. An unforgettable phenomenon!

Another cameo:

The boys of the Youth Club that haven't been able to get away come to see me as they hear I am back. I am under no illusions about them but I love them. Maybe one or two of them will over-come the inclination to laziness and make something of his life. Generally I do not put much reliance on them; they are just too satisfied to scrounge pocket money from their fathers or their older brothers who are working.

Yet they come in with stories of personal courage. Fleeing like everyone else towards Wazirabad, they are stopped at the first canal by soldiers. The canal security guards climb on the buses and yell out "All Christians on the bus get off!" There is a widespread hysteria that Christians, because decades ago most of their forebears have emerged out of Hinduism, are now actively engaged in spying for India.

It could have been that other passengers on the bus might have been able to identify some of them as Christians. From their appearance however it would have been difficult to do so. Yet I hear of none of our boys who fail to get up from his seat and shuffle off the bus through the crowded passengers. As they dis-mount they are beaten with blows over the shoulders from raised rifle butts. "You scum! Get back into Sialkot and wait there until your Indian masters come to settle up with you!" More blows and beatings ensue.

Against the onrushing tide of frightened people they have walked the long miles back home. They are learning the hard way that to be a Christian is to be treated as an alien in your own country.

Letters from Sialkot

September 1965

Marie has kept these two letters of mine from Sialkot to the boys in Murree. They have been found amongst her papers.

September 16th, 1965

Dear Timmy,

The guns are sounding nearer and to the south. I am thinking a lot about you this morning while you are in school struggling over spellings and arithmetic.

Daddy and Mummy love you so very much. You are a very special little boy to both of us. You have given us delight in SO many ways. We are both lucky to have such a lovely son. We love the way your imagination takes fire at an idea and you have shared so many lovely and sweet thoughts with us both.

In these days, while Mummy is worried and concerned I know you will be her comfort in a very special way. You are young, even though you are now eight, but you are very responsible and upright. Tell Mummy she should put her trust in God for worrying is sin – and be in the Peace Jesus gives to us. If you do not hear news of Daddy for some while then you must lead Mummy through the

Book of Psalms and underline for her all the precious
promises there.
The psalm I have chosen for you yourself is Psalm 91.

He that dwelleth in the secret place of the most High
shall abide under the shadow of the Almighty.
I will say to the Lord,
He is my refuge and my fortress;
my God; in him will I trust.
Surely he shall deliver thee from the snare of the fowler,
and from the noisome pestilence.
He shall cover thee with his feathers,
and under his wings shalt thou trust;
his truth shall be thy shield and buckler.
Thou shalt not be afraid for the terror by night;
nor for the arrow that flieth by day;
Nor for the pestilence that walketh in darkness;
nor for the destruction that wasteth at noonday.
A thousand shall fall at thy side,
and ten thousand at thy right hand;
but it shall not come nigh thee.
Only with thine eyes shalt thou behold
and see the reward of the wicked.
Because thou hast made the Lord,
which is my refuge,
even the most High, thy habitation;
There shall no evil befall thee,
neither shall any plague come nigh thy dwelling.
For he shall give his angels charge over thee,
to keep thee in all thy ways.
They shall bear thee up in their hands,
lest thou dash thy foot against a stone.

Thou shalt tread upon the lion and adder;
the young lion and the dragon shalt thou trample under feet.
Because he hath set his love upon me,
therefore will I deliver him;
I will set him on high,
because he hath known my name.
He shall call upon me, and I will answer him;
I will be with him in trouble;
I will deliver him, and honour him.
With long life will I satisfy him,
and shew him my salvation.

What lovely pictures of protection this psalm gives to us.
'a secret hiding place'   *–verse 1*
'in God's shadow'   *–verse 1*
'a fortress or castle'   *–verse 2*
'a little creature of the woods
   being protected from traps'   *–verse 3*
'like a mother hen guarding her chickens' *–verse 4*
'an angel standing guard over us'   *–verse 4*
'a shield'   *–verse 4*
and so on through the psalm.
God take care of you, Timbo Bimbo, and remember –
NEVER tell a lie, even if it hurts.

Lots of Love, Daddy

11 a.m. September 16th, 1965

Dear Colin Bollin,

Daddy has been thinking a lot about you and Mummy and Timmy as the guns have sounded closer and closer today. I know you will be a great comfort to Mummy while things are so uncertain.

Today I sent Shah Zaman and his family off by bus to Rawalpindi and Taxila. They took Jack the dog with them and I brought Puff back here. When Shah Zaman is settled then he will come back to Murree to see you all.

I went over to see Aunty May Scott and Aunty Elizabeth and Uncle Malcolm at Barahpatthar today and told them I thought they should move to Gujrat with the teachers and girls they have left (about twenty) so I'll find out tomorrow what they decide to do.

I have also decided to go over to Hajipura to sleep each night for a while to be with Aunty Anne and Aunty Piri and the seventeen little babies and Uncle Edward and our student nurses.

Now we are all trusting in Jesus, pray each night for all of us here in Sialkot and our friends all over the world who are worried about us.

Mummy and I are so proud of you and as you grow up we begin to see the kind of boy, and man, you will be. We pray that you will grow up to be honest and truthful, to help others, to work hard and encourage those in trouble. We love you very much and as I write I feel I am putting my arms around you and holding you tight.

You can be a real help to me by the way you look after

Mummy now, how you quickly answer when Mummy asks instead of pretending not to hear and just being good. I have a psalm for you. It is the 121st Psalm.

> I will lift up mine eyes unto the hills,
> from whence cometh my help.
> My help cometh from the Lord,
> which made heaven and earth.
> He will not suffer thy foot to be moved;
> he that keepeth thee will not slumber.
> Behold, he that keepeth Israel
> shall neither slumber nor sleep.
> The Lord is thy keeper;
> The Lord is thy shade upon thy right hand.
> The sun shall not smite thee by day,
> nor the moon by night.
> The Lord shall preserve thee from all evil;
> he shall preserve thy soul.
> The Lord shall preserve thy going out and thy coming in
> from this time forth, and even for evermore.

This is the psalm people in Sialkot sing with tears in their eyes as someone leaves them – it is a psalm I learned at your age and that I hope you will learn too.

All my love, Daddy

Colin, Ken, Marie and Tim

Peter

Taxila, December 1966

In England the three large prefabricated buildings that I have ordered for the operating block at Taxila and the two eye-wards are under preparation but have not yet been shipped. I am involved in the preparatory site work, including the foundations that I can prepare ahead of time.

Our two boys are now nine years old and have come down from boarding school with Dr. Lall's oldest son, Sunil, during the first week of December. The Christy kids usually also come to Taxila but have gone down to Sialkot where their parents are covering for the absence of the Hamms. It is so good to have the boys home. Their two Samoyed puppies, Husky and Piskey, turn cartwheels with delight. For only three months in each year is it possible for them to be with us at home on the plains and lead normal family lives.

For the boys it is a different home than the one they had left. Before Marie returns from Murree at the end of the summer I move from the Mission Hospital in Sialkot to the bungalow in Taxila where Marie and Mac had once lived. Although Tim has lived in Taxila before, Colin has not.

Marie is plainly disappointed I have done no sorting and selecting of the furnishings and other junk before trucking it back up north. I am more sure than she that we will ultimately find use for those bamboo curtains that we have possessed for ten years and never used. (We never do.) She is outspoken in amazement at some of the items she is still having to store.

Christmas is going to be busy. We have three young men from Gordon College in Rawalpindi, an Englishman and two Scots who are going to be visiting just over the Christmas / New Year period.

We also have Peter.

Dr. Ernest Lall has brought over to us early in the month a letter from a stranger in Peshawar, an English surgeon, who is planning to come to Taxila Hospital for a visit. It has been recommended that he should see the eye work while he is in Pakistan.

We smile over the letter. The writer asks if we can book him into a local hotel for the period of his short stay. Any hotels that Taxila might possess will be little more than rented string beds, without mattresses, and probably out in the open. Marie takes the letter and replies to it. We will meet him at the station when he arrives.

We have not previously had any guest like Peter. Peter is best described as the typical English gentleman. Imagine a late middle-aged man, tall, graying hair, kindly face with all the courtesies and customs and, yes, the chivalry, of the English upper class. We bid him welcome, bring him up to the house, give him tea and settle him in one of the guest rooms. We let the boys tell him about themselves, bubbling and giggling with laughter, until it is mealtime.

Peter is fascinated with our home, its mere daily routine. He seems almost more interested in the way Marie manages her household and Khan Zaman the kitchen than in the work in the crowded hospital. It is an orderly household even with two exuberant little boys. Early rising. Everyone gathers around the meal-table at the same time and is included in meal-table conversations. Grace is said before meals and daily activities include family devotions. Kindness and courtesy abound with never a cross word; there is much laughter. Nothing particularly pious, just normal routine.

He is particularly anxious never to miss morning or evening devotions.

Marie and I like Peter immensely. He is clearly a good and kind man but, equally clearly, in some inner way he is deeply troubled. There is a burden—a shadow—that he is carrying. He will no doubt tell us in good time if he so wishes. He does tell us a little about himself. He is married and has two married daughters. He is concerned about the health of his grandson who has an inherited physical defect that could be life threatening. He is clearly wealthy.

He is a senior surgeon at one of the major provincial hospitals within the British National Health Service. He has taken up at the spur of the moment an invitation of a younger acquaintance who is now a missionary doctor in Peshawar. However Alex Barclay is not in Peshawar when he arrives, so he has come on down to Taxila.

Later we become aware that Peter's journey is a response to counsel from his vicar, Os Guinness, who has told him, "What you need to do, Peter, quite simply, is to go away somewhere, a long way away, and find God. Take whatever time you need."

Peter eventually feels that he has imposed himself enough upon his Taxila hosts and that he needs to move on. He has an arrangement to go tiger hunting with the British Ambassador in Delhi. Marie urges Peter to stay longer, to stay over Christmas. If not, then he should know as he journeys on that he will be welcome here if ever he should decide to come back. He is family and we will be here for him.

We, boys and all, are sad to see him go. We feel that he is still a troubled man and we long to help him. In the guest book, on the 9th of December, as he departs he writes simply, "What a wonderful home!"

On December the 15th we have a phone call from Peter. Peter cannot have learned that in Pakistan you only ever try to make phone calls as a last resort and inevitably it requires many attempts and much patience. We never normally had a phone in our house and saved ourselves much frustration but there is a phone in the Taxila house because this is usually a doctor's home.

"I am wondering whether I might accept your kind invitation and come back?"

"Of course, Peter, we'll be delighted, where are you speaking from?"

I assume it is New Delhi. It isn't. It is Rawalpindi!

"Oh, just go outside, Peter and take a taxi, you can be here in about forty minutes, your bed is ready and supper is at six."

When the boys are in bed Peter tells us his story. He is so relieved to be back, it is as though a great burden has rolled off his shoulders. Perhaps we have guessed. He is an alcoholic. He has been fighting it for years but there is no way out of it. It is getting worse, not better. He has taken his vicar's advice but Alec Barclay is in Kabul so he has visited Taxila. In New Delhi he has gone on a binge of drinking in his hotel room and there is only one place left for him to go. He wants to discover how people can be as happy as we are without a drop of drink in the house.

Just a few miles up the road a Muslim woman is having her own search for God.

They will meet and walk parallel for a while.

Peter too will find Him, in his own less dramatic way and become later an answer to our own prayers.

Damascus Way

Heavens exulting
Tempests tumulting
Oceans turmoiling
Hills about falling,
Waves above breaking
Sky and earth shaking
Trumpets like thunder
Clouds burst asunder
Chariots blazing
Flames wildly raging

Bright beyond bearing
Burnished and searing
Holy designing
Focused and shining
Stabbing and piercing
Burning, releasing
Savaged by splendour
Purged of all anger
All fear and all pain
Born naked again.
Eye of God seeking
Voice of God speaking
Dawn of God breaking
Sword of God striking
Hand of God pointing
Oil for anointing
Glory gold glowing
Streaming and flowing
A great shining sea –
oh, no, Lord, not me!

Marie, Ken and Bilquis

Meeting Bilquis

The next portion of the book follows the spiritual journey of a remarkable woman. Marie and I felt afterwards that although we had come to Taxila to build an operating block at the hospital, that God's real purpose for us was different. He purposed that we be given the opportunity to observe close hand what happens when a soul becomes given over to God and that we be privileged to play a small part in that journey.

For us the story begins on Boxing Day in the year 1966.

Christmas is so much fun this year. Roger is a violinist so we have all kinds of crazy and not so crazy music. Timmy knocks the

piano about; Colin is learning to play the clarinet. Dave and Synnove Mitchell who live in the Wah Cement Factory employee's
quarters come and join us for Christmas Eve. Their two children
increase the party. The Mitchells are a musical family. We have a
noisy time of games, fun, food and presents just like any Christmas family anywhere.

We missionaries are fortunate that we do not live in a western world of prepared entertainment. We have never wanted television and the radio is only for the news (and the international
cricket Test Matches). Marie and I may have taken the boys to
the movies perhaps four times over the years we are here. We do
have long playing classical records and we do have books. Most
missionary families have brought with them any musical instruments they would require. We are fortunate to acquire a piano.
Entertainment, whatever it is to be, will be self-created. We play
board games, questions around the table and never seem to lack
for things to do.

The Mitchells are in TEAM Mission, neighbors who have
taken over part of the Sialkot Mission territory to the north and
west. Dave and I are sharing responsibilities for a regular Sunday evening English language service. This meeting is usually in
our house at the hospital. Other than missionaries, their visitors
and Ernest and Pramila who are doctors at the hospital, Pakistani
Christians from the cantonment attend. Marie and I usually also
have a midweek Bible Study in Wah Cantonment in the home of
Pakistani Christian friends.

Synnove is from Norway so, like Marie also, Scandinavian.
Scandinavians celebrate Christmas and the opening of gifts on
Christmas Eve. Christmas Day is a quieter worshipful occasion.
She and David will be sharing in the community meal in Hasan
Abdal. All of us remaining in Taxila will be sharing in the tradi-
tional dinner outside on the lawn for all the hospital staff. The

first of the winter rains has not yet come and there seems little threat of it to spoil the occasion

Boxing Day, the day after Christmas Day, seems to be a peculiarly English celebration. Synnove, as she leaves for home, invites us all to a return visit at her home on Boxing Day. She has invited Mrs. Sheikh who is living in our old home in Wah village to come also. Synnove is unsure whether Bilquis will indeed come.

We have seen Mrs. Sheikh before on one or two occasions as we have been driving on our way down to Wah Gardens and she has been on the roadside at her house. We have never spoken to her. She has given us the impression of a hard woman, an unhappy woman who will not welcome greetings from passing strangers and we have driven on without pausing.

Now however, in and amongst the Christmas decorations and the loaded table of the Mitchell's humble home our eyes are fixed upon her with a different understanding and we are not missing a word of what she says. Her first name, Bilquis, reputed to have been the first name of the Queen of Sheba, is pronounced as you would pronounce the name Bill Keece. Let me describe her as we came to know her.

Bilquis is a woman of average height, a year or so older than Marie and of graceful carriage. She has a full face with widely pitched eyes and a ready smile, the light brown complexion of Pakistanis. She laughs easily and has a ready sense of humor. She has a husky voice, perfect English with a broad vocabulary and only a slight accent. She is poised and self-controlled. She wears both sari and shalwarqamiz with an easy grace. I don't recall ever seeing her in western clothes. Frequently in her own home she will be barefoot. Her hair is jet black tending to touches of gray. She has large brown eyes.

There is an openness to her; you don't feel this is a closed-in private person masking her feelings and emotions. She is welcoming you into the intimacy of a heart friendship without reservations.

She loves beautiful things, savors the nuances of perfume, pauses to let the beauty of miniatures, buds and flowers, jewelry take their transience into the inner eternity of her heart. Particularly she loves gardens. If where she lives there is no garden, she will create one, blending a harmony of flowers and grasses, shrubs and bushes. At her home in Peniel, on the edge of Wah village, there is also flowing water and she creates her own little paradise where sound and scent as well as sight blend to perfection.

You recognize at once this is a woman born to authority and accustomed to being in control of her situation. She has *presence* or *robe* as we call it. Her mind is clear and incisive, her questions immediately beyond the superficial. She wastes little time on the long courtesies of trivia in greeting or farewell, seeking instead, while still polite, to be expressing and listening or responding to things that really concern her.

The focus of her human love is her grandchild and adopted son, Mahmud. She treats her servants feudally, in the best sense of that word. She doesn't exploit them; they are very junior members of her household family. She expects and receives obedience. She says candidly she does their thinking for them. She also helps them with their medical bills, their marriages and their funerals; all are part and parcel of one active ménage with Bilquis at its head. Servants give loyalty and there is a generous loyalty given in return.

She is a passionate woman, supporter of causes (particularly the rights of women) and an active advocate for those causes she believes in. She is courageous and rarely shows fear, more usually a strange composure drawn from depths within her. She would have despised cowardice in others and in herself. In spiritual matters she is intense and focused. In much of her conversation on spiritual things she speaks with awe in her voice. Because she is accustomed to authority she accepts authority, the authority of the Holy Spirit. Once she is clear in her mind about the Holy Spirit's direction for her life or actions then likely adverse consequences are an irrelevance.

Almost from the beginning she seems to enjoy that platform of *abiding* that Paul describes as *"being seated together with Christ in heavenly places"* except that she would have seen herself not seated but as the woman washing his feet with her tears and wiping them with her hair.

Narayan Tilak wrote a hymn, now in our Western hymnbooks that, like no other hymn I know, catches the spirit of the broken heart of India as it encounters Christ. It begins

One who is all unfit to count as scholar in Thy school
Thou, of Thy love, hast made a friend, O Love most wonderful!

Each of the verses catches the brokenness of the Unworthy before the perfection of the Unsoiled. That is Bilquis.

A Bible for Bilquis

December 26, 1966

Bilquis is obviously full of something, something very important to her that she is anxious to share. Synnove quiets her down and persuades her to be patient. She completes the introductions, tells Bilquis firmly that until everyone has a cup of tea in their hands there is no way she can share her news because she, Synnove, wants to sit and listen to her too. Meanwhile she can fill in the background as to what has been happening to her.

Very quickly, as Synnove busies herself with hostess duties, Bilquis tells of her background. The Hayat family has held Wah village for more than seven hundred years. She is one of that family. Her uncle has been Prime Minister of the Punjab in British days and her father a Government minister. Her husband, an army general, has been Minister of the Interior during the recent martial law period under President Ayub Khan. She herself has had a senior position in the Women's Army Corps before the Raj ended and has been a foreign correspondent for London's Kemsley Newspapers. She has also been adviser to the President on women's affairs. Her marriage breaks up when her husband leaves her.

After her divorce she has retreated from public life and has come to live in her brother Mahmud's cottage. She has three children. Only Munawwar (Tooni) lives nearby, working part-time as the company doctor for an oil company halfway between Wah and Rawalpindi. Munawwar has one son, named after her favorite uncle, Mahmud.

Tooni's own marriage has been unhappy and eventually it is also to end in divorce. As they work out their differences both parents ask Bilquis if she will keep their one-year old baby for a while. Bilquis, however, can see seeds of continuing conflict in this proposal. The child will become a shuttlecock between two adversaries.

She declines but offers instead to adopt the little boy legally and raise him as her own son. The parents agree to this although Bilquis is unclear quite what the situation will be when the boy reaches the age of seven. The father has the right to make choices concerning his education and, probably, his future care and career.

Mahmud is now four. He is clearly the apple of Bilquis's eye. Her world revolves about him. She cannot bear the thought of ever losing him. They live together in Wah Cottage beside the Dhamra Bridge together with several servants who take care of them. Their life is a happy one. Tooni visits her son and mother regularly.

Having painted in quickly the background to her life she now begins to fill in the drama of the past couple of months. Synnove is settled and the house quiet except for Bilquis speaking. The series of *encounters and experiences* has begun two months previously in October.

First, while walking in the garden as night fell she has felt *something* brush past her and then *something unseen* tap her hand. That scares and unsettles her.

Then a day or so later Mahmud has fallen sick and lost his appetite. Bilquis has called the Wah maulvi to the cottage to pray for Mahmud. She has not been impressed with his knowledge or his prayers. She will read the Q'ran herself and do her own praying.

Bilquis does not count herself a religious woman although she lives and operates as far as possible within the permissible parameters of Islam. She is not out to flaunt any disagreement she might feel with the ordained place of women within Islam. Rather she is now rereading the Q'ran with a distinct desire to discover within it the voice of God for her. However as she reads, as the references to Jesus make clear that he was without sin and born of a virgin, she finds herself wondering whether, in addition to the Q'ran, she should not also be reading the Bible.

The form of the Q'ran is revelation. It is Allah revealing His Will for men and women by the angel messenger Gabriel to His Last Chosen Prophet, Muhammed. Implicitly it is less easy to understand than a narrative which creates a flow of mental pictures to carry the reader along.

Nagging her mind now, even while she reads, is the insistent thought that in addition to reading the Q'ran she should also be reading the Bible. She is aware that the Bible is a record of God's dealings with the Jews and, later, Christians. She has been told that the book has been deliberately altered to make the record of events fit the editors' own beliefs.

She asks both of her Christian servants, Raisham, her maidservant and Manzur, her driver to bring her a Bible. Days pass. It is not forthcoming. Finally she gives Manzur an order "Go right now and get me a Bible!"

It arrives, unseen and unannounced, upon her table. It is written in an archaic Urdu form. She picks it up. She opens it at random seeking a chance verse to see what it might say to her. Her eye is drawn immediately to a verse in the lower right hand corner that seems illuminated on the page:

> *I will call them my people, which were not my people;*
> *and her beloved, which was not beloved.*
>
> *—Romans 9:25*

What does that mean?

She slips a card in the place where the book is open. When the house has quieted, Mahmud is asleep and she is alone she opens the book again, rereads that verse and then reads on, slowly and thoughtfully, trying to make sense of affirmations that cut across a lifetime's understanding.

> *Here I lay in Zion a stone to trip over,*
> *a rock to stumble against;*
> *But he who has faith in him*
> *will not be put to shame.*
>
> *—Romans 9:33 NEB*

> *For Christ ends the Law*
> *and brings righteousness*
> *for everyone who has faith.*
>
> *—Romans 10:4 NEB*

> *If on your lips is the confession, 'Jesus is Lord,'*
> *and in your heart the faith that God raised him from the*
> *dead, then you will find salvation.*
>
> *—Romans 10:9 NEB*

This is teaching in clear contradiction to the Q'ran Sharif. What is she to make of it?

Events are moving steadily forward, events she can't pretend to understand. Normally she does not dream and she is not given to fantasizing.

That night she dreams of having a meal with Jesus. Imprinted on her mind on waking are the words *John The Baptist*.

"I look in the index to the Bible. There are four books attributed to John. The three shorter ones are letters, very good letters for certain but they don't appear to have been written by John the Baptist. The fourth book in the New Testament is also called John. Although John the Baptist is not mentioned by name there is a man called John who is baptizing. This is probably who John the Baptist is but I will need some help to understand what my dream means.

"That evening I have Manzur, my driver, get the car out. He is surprised that I do not want him to drive me. I tell him I am not going far but do not say where I am going. I drive across the bridge towards Hasan Abdal to the home of David and Synnove Mitchell. I must find answers to my questions and they are missionaries.

"I have never been there before and Mrs. Mitchell is surprised to see me. She invites me in and offers me a cup of tea or coffee but I decline, I have not come for coffee but to ask a question or two if this is a convenient time.

"I ask her to tell me all she knows about John the Baptist. She tells me that she really knows little about him except that he has come to prepare the way for Jesus Christ. So I ask her to tell me all she knows about Jesus and she does."

Learning to Pray

Bilquis has been telling us of her first visit to Synnove. Peter is drinking in every word. He is on the same journey as Bilquis though, like the rest of us, worlds behind this woman who has suddenly burst ahead of us all. The children too are listening carefully, seated on the floor leaning against their parents' legs. You can hear a pin drop.

"When Synnove tells me about Jesus I begin to glimpse that perhaps there is another way in which the world and life and everything in it makes sense. Such thoughts, though only seeds, are radical and dangerous. I will need time.

"Now I share with her what has been happening at the Cottage. I ask her to pray for me and she does. We both kneel on her floor and she prays a simple prayer straight from her heart. As I leave to return home I ask her whether there is any connection between Jesus and perfume. I have had a strange dream about a perfume salesman and when I awoke the beautiful perfume persisted in the room. Later I smelled it again in the garden. She could not think of any connection at that moment.

"The following day she sends me a note giving a reference in the Bible;

> *But thanks be to God, who continually leads us about,*
> *captives in Christ's triumphal procession,*
> *and everywhere uses us to reveal and spread abroad*

the fragrance of the knowledge of himself!
We are indeed the incense offered by Christ to God,
. . . a vital fragrance that brings life.
—*2 Corinthians 2:14–17 NEB*

"David has been away in Peshawar and Afghanistan so when he returns Synnove brings him around to the Cottage to meet me. I am reading both the Q'ran of my childhood and the Bible and my questions are mounting. I am finding too that the key to the peace in my heart is related to what I am reading.

"My peace though is suddenly disturbed. Mahmud becomes ill with an ear ailment. I check him in to the Holy Family Hospital in Pindi for a thorough checkup. Tooni is working there so things are easy to arrange. Dr. Pia, a Filipino nun, is Superintendent. She notices my Bible when she visits our private room. I tell her I am earnestly searching for God but that He seems so . . . so remote, so distant. Her answer staggers me. I should pray to Him as though He were my father.

"That thought keeps ricocheting around my mind. It will not let me go. No ailment is discovered with Mahmud, the symptoms disappear as mysteriously as they have come. We return to Wah but that thought is now ever with me. God is like my father? My father and I have had a wonderful relationship. We have been so close. God is like my father?

"Suddenly, one night, about a fortnight ago, well after midnight, I decide to take Dr. Pia's advice. I slip out of bed and kneel beside it. I speak to God. I call Him Father. At first I am hesitant and then I become more bold. "Father, O Father, O Father, my Father, Father God"—the words, once released, are tumbling over themselves and I know that, in some amazing way, He is hearing me. I don't need to understand how it is happening, it is simple absolute certain truth and complete joy that He is hearing me.

That is enough—God, Holy God, is hearing me! I am His child. He is my Father!

"It is so comforting, so 'warm' to be in His presence. I am crying, talking to Him through my tears. I am so sorry! So sorry for so many things! Can He forgive me? I lay my whole life before Him. Forgive me, Father. I have hurt so many people! Forgive me, Father. I have been so willful, so self-centered. Forgive me, Father. I need Him so much, forgive me, Father.

"For three glorious penitent heart-cleansing hours my Father and I have fellowship together. I know that from henceforth my guide will have to be the book where God is revealed as my Father, whatever the consequences. Whatever the consequences?

"In the cold light of ensuing days, even while I am reading steadily through the New Testament I am thinking about the consequences. I am suddenly realizing that we do not live unto ourselves, that we are not islands. Each of us is a center, the center of our own peculiar world. What happens to us is of immense importance to others. Acts of our own freewill have consequences, often severe consequences affecting others. Those others are not remote and far away but those nearest and dearest to us. We with the best of intentions can cause pain and suffering to those we would most desire to protect from pain and suffering.

"Perhaps I can handle the shame of association with 'sweeper Christians'—'bhangis'—but can those I love? Perhaps I can handle the religious reaction of a proud family suddenly brought to public shame but is it fair on them? Can I cope with my children's response, and the effect upon their lives? Maybe worst of all, can I face the loss of Mahmud? Is it even right to put him, and his whole life at risk? And is putting my own life at risk fair to him?

"I pack up my things and take Mahmud into Pindi for a wild spree of shopping. I know I am running away and recognize after several days it is not possible. This is something I cannot run away from. I have to face it. I come back home.

"Mahmud is in bed asleep. There is a fire in the fireplace and I sit beside it, reading.

"I read right through the New Testament and am now into the last book. Suddenly a verse catches my attention."

> Here I stand knocking at the door;
> if anyone hears my voice and opens the door,
> I will come in and sit down to supper with him and he
> with me.
> —Revelation 3:20 NEB

"This is my dream! Jesus is standing at the door. He is standing there now! I have choices to make. He will not force his company upon me. The dream is from God and it is directed to me.

"I have a choice to make. I make it.

"I kneel before the fire. I speak to my Father and I speak to Jesus. 'Come into my heart. Come now. Whatever the consequences, come now.'

"Quite simply, He came and I know He came."

All is not yet done. There is one transaction more.

"I know nothing of the Holy Spirit except as I have read. I know though that I need the Holy Spirit too, that my experience of God will be incomplete without Him. Jesus has promised to send Him. Peter and the others had received Him; Paul had spoken frequently of Him.

"As I drift off to sleep I commit this need to my Father and to Jesus His Son who has promised it.

"I awake at 3 a.m. The night air is cold, the fire long out.

"I slip to my knees beside the bed and begin to claim the Holy Spirit for myself.

"As I look up I seem to be looking into a great light. I am crying, desperate for the complete revelation that the New Testament assures me is promised.

"Father," I cry, "You gave the Holy Spirit to Peter and to John and the others and they had already known Jesus, they had talked to Him and they had touched Him and yet You gave the Holy Spirit to them. They didn't need Him as much as I do. I never had that opportunity, I need the Holy Spirit so much more and I am not going to get up from this place until you give it to me. Father, You have to give it to me. I know You love me and You have to give it to me. I'm your child."

Bilquis looks around at each of us slowly. "It was as though the very doors of heaven opened and I saw His Face. Suddenly I was bathed in an onrushing heavenly love that totally surrounded me and surged through me. I was totally caught up in wonder and praise and light and the glory of heaven. Whatever dross was in me was washed away and I desperately longed that these moments of superlative joy sweeping like waves over me might go on and on and on and never end. I was experiencing heaven.

"I do not know how long the experience lasted. I became conscious of my surroundings only as the first traces of dawn lit the sky."

"Bilquis," I ask, like all the other listeners deeply moved and very curious, "when you were praising God what language were you praising Him in?"

Not only can Bilquis use the languages of English, Urdu and Punjabi fluently but it seems likely she has been using a heavenly language. This would have been a language she read of in the letters of Paul but which she has never heard spoken. She can't remember. The whole experience has been graphic and transcendent and the language of her praise she can't remember.

It has happened two days previously, on Christmas Eve!

Bilquis and Marie

1966 / 67

Bilquis, in a most wonderful way by the presentation of a compliant heart, has made her basic spiritual commitments under the hand of God with little counsel from others. Although she quickly responds to urgings to commit herself to fellowship with others, this is really for much of her Christian life a struggle for her. Her most precious moments continue throughout her life to be those alone with her Lord. Although she retains close and dear personal Christian friends she finds difficulty, other than the Taxila English service, in locating a congregation where she can worship and be fed without being a curiosity.

Marie and I visit Bilquis at her cottage during that last week of the year. There is an immediate affinity and we have an opportunity to visit our old home. Tim and Colin go off with Mahmud to see his Christmas toys, his grandmother has been extravagant.

While they are playing we tell Bilquis of the Sunday evening service in our home at the hospital and of the Wednesday Bible Study we have in Sheila and Taj's home in Wah cantonment. We urge her to participate in both. Somehow it seems to be God's method to nourish our spiritual growth within the framework of a worshipping community even though we might prefer to travel alone. It is also wise to set aside time to study the Bible together with others in a group, we can benefit from each other's insights and we will develop in a balanced way.

When we find that Bilquis is using a King James version of the Bible to study from Timmy happily hands over to Bilquis his more modern version of the Bible.

I also share a concern much impressed upon my heart. This experience of Bilquis is not for her alone. God is blessing her so that by sharing she might later bless others. That will work itself out in due course but it is essential for now that she maintain a daily journal of her Father's dealings with her. That should include her questions as well as her insights and notes of her daily circumstances, her disappointments and discouragements as well as her joys and surprises.

She agrees to do so and whenever we meet she brings out her journal and we go through her recent experiences together.

Possibly the Sunday after Christmas is the first time she has ever been to a Christian service although perhaps in the Army or in England or France she might have ventured into a church. Certainly however this is Bilquis's first encounter as a Christian with a Christian congregation. It is a crowded living room although there are only a dozen or so of us: Doctors Ernest and Pramila Lall from the hospital, Peter and our visitors, our family, several Pakistani friends I pick up from the cantonment, the Mitchells and Bilquis.

The first hymn we sing she sings with tears running down her cheeks.

> I know not why God's wondrous Grace
> To me He hath made known
> Nor why unworthy as I am
> He claimed me for His own
> But I know whom I have believed

And am persuaded that He is able
To keep that which I've committed
Unto Him against that day.

As we look across and see the broken contrite tears of this imperious woman laying her own life on the line in a way none of us have ever had to, few of us can restrain our own tears.

There develops over the next several months a wonderful warmth of relationship between Bilquis, full of questions and Marie, full of sound common sense and practical goodness and counsel. They are of an age, enjoy each other's company and both share the alien English custom of good piping hot tea in bone china cups poured from a similar teapot cradled in an appliquéd tea cozy with silver spoons, lace doilies and linen napkins to make the serving complete. Bilquis is writing letters to us constantly, full of the most beautiful childlike simplicity on the one hand and the deep searching questions of a mature believing mind on the other.

She writes with an unmistakable mannish hand but it is easy to recognize the intrinsic spiritual value of these records of the journey of a soul towards the light of God. We keep them all.

When we aren't meeting for midweek Bible study in her home or on Sunday evenings at Taxila Marie visits Wah Cottage with the boys so that the three young friends can have time together to play while the two women spend time in sharing and prayer. It is easier for Bilquis to visit the hospital than to draw attention to herself by visiting the Mitchells: Bilquis is soon almost a daily visitor. Opposition is developing within the family and there are many matters for prayer.

Bilquis is working her way through Matthew. It is a delight to sit with her and observe the searchlight of a sharp clear penetrating mind playing on familiar passages of Scripture with complete faith and trust and a strong desire to know their meaning. We are beginning to see how familiarity dulls our perceptions.

> *Jesus called a little child unto him*
> *and said,*
> *Verily I say unto you*
> *Except ye be converted*
> *And become as little children*
> *Ye shall not enter into*
> *The kingdom of heaven.*
> *Whosoever therefore shall humble himself*
> *As this little child,*
> *The same is greatest*
> *In the kingdom of heaven*
>
> *—Matthew 18:2–4*

Bilquis needs to fathom this. How does anyone humble himself or herself? What is humility? We explore this together. How can she pretend that her servants are as good as she is? She has a trained mind. She has centuries of ancestry that equip her for her role. She does their thinking for them. She and they are much better off that she is doing it for them rather than their trying to do it themselves. They haven't been taught to think. Is the Father saying she should sit on the floor with them and say they are equal to her when they so obviously are not?

Gradually our spirited conversations agree that humility is not involved with comparing one person with another. Humility is not the idea that some other is better in some way than I. It is rather myself seen from God's perspective and God seen from my perspective. This makes total sense to Bilquis. This is a humility she can understand.

It is a humility that in relation to God she already possesses. Is it possible to work out for herself the consequences of that kind of love for God in her relationships with others?

One Wednesday we come across to Bilquis early. As we come down the steps beside the house we hear singing, the familiar Punjabi rendering, in men's voices, of the twenty-fourth Psalm. What is going on? We pause at the door a few moments before we slip off our shoes and join Bilquis. She is being visited by a Punjabi Christian singing party, perhaps from the little church at Hasan Abdal a couple of miles away. There are maybe five or six of them, all men. The usual musical instruments are there, the harmonium, the dholki, the tabla and the chimta. The lips of the lead singer are stained with betel juice and his teeth are broken and uneven. A scarf is wrapped loosely around his head. His voice is high-pitched and searing, the chorus accompanied by the rhythmic clap of the others present. Several of the party's womenfolk are also present, each head covered with the draped dopatta. In with them is Raisham, Bilquis' Christian maidservant. All present are sitting cross-legged on the floor. Among them, similarly head-covered, smiling and happy, nodding to us to join her is Bilquis!

Bilquis wants communion. On Wednesday afternoons before we collect the others and start our Bible Study, she asks, "Couldn't the three of us have communion together?" Jesus had said when establishing the sacrament *Do this in remembrance of me.* He had died for her and she wishes to remember Him. I tell her I'd better check first. Although I am not a Presbyterian by birth I am now a Presbyterian missionary so should abide by the rules of the Presbyterian Church. I write to Wilbur Christy, the Principal of the Theological Seminary in Gujranwala. He is the doyen of our Sialkot Mission remnant. Wilbur is understanding but "No!" I need to be ordained first. I'm not even an elder.

I explain to Bilquis that I cannot serve her with communion because the rules of my church do not permit me to do so. However I know of no rule to bar me from participating in communion offered to me by someone who is not a Presbyterian. Her eyes twinkle. Her serving Marie and me communion seems somehow to fit right in with the unusual circumstances that govern recent events at Peniel. She always officiates in the ceremony of remembrance with solemnity and reverence.

A Double Baptism

It is almost one month since we first met Bilquis. It is also exactly one month since she has had her encounter with the Holy Spirit at Peniel. She drives into the hospital much earlier than usual, about 8 a.m., pulls up in front of our house and hurries inside.

I have already set my laborers to work and Nur Zaman, my foreman, can see to the rest of the day. I know I have to tell Bilquis right away of the night's happenings. Somehow we have to arrange immediately for her baptism. There will be no time to waste. Marie is preparing tea for the three of us in the kitchen and Bilquis is standing with her. She is upset and flustered. Her eyes are anxious. "Ken," she turns to me as soon as I come into the kitchen looking for the two women "I have to be baptized today, I just have to, the Lord is telling me it must be done today and I mustn't wait."

I smile.

"Come in and sit down, Bilquis. Of course you are going to be baptized today. God has been telling me too. Listen to what happened during the night."

Slowly I take her through a nocturnal encounter I have had that night. I have heard a voice and its instruction to turn to page 456 in my Bible. I turn to the page, Job 13 and 14, and show her the references and read them slowly to her. When I read, "*Though*

He slay me, yet will I trust in Him" she nods her head affirmatively. Her anxiety now is all gone. Things are moving at last. The Lord has taken a hand!

"It's all a question now of the arrangements for your baptism. I'll go over and talk to Padri Gulab Khan."

I find him in his quarters. I love this old man, himself a convert, gloriously humble and wonderfully faithful. He is prepared to baptize Bilquis even though there might be angry consequences but first he will need to obtain the approval of the church session. I throw up my hands. That will never work. That could take days! I thank the pastor and hurry back to the house. Bilquis and Marie are waiting.

"Let's go to the Mitchell's right away, we'll sort out something. We'll take our car as well in case we need to separate." We tell Tim and Colin we will soon be back and leave them in Peter's charge.

We just catch David and Synnove, they are about to head to Abbottabad for a committee meeting of their Mission. They listen to us. Yes, the Lord's directions are plain to us all. Bilquis needs to be baptized right away and we will just have to let God take care of the consequences. Unfortunately they have to be away so they will be unable to help but they will concur wholeheartedly in anything we are able to arrange.

"Dave, you go to Abbottabad and find somebody there who will baptize Bilquis. We will be there at 2:30 this afternoon and we'll have the baptism then. Where will you be?" Dave blinks, looks at our earnest faces and gulps. It is all right for Ken to say that but . . . all he can think of is problems immediately ahead but well, the Lord is clearly speaking so there must be some answers out there somewhere. They better get started on their way.

We drop Bilquis off at her house; we will pick her up at 12:30

and bring Colin and Tim to play with Mahmud until we get back. We should be back before dark.

We invite Peter to come along with us. This gentle thoughtful man is trying to make his own sense of what is happening around him. What kind of Christianity is this? Here is a woman of exceptional intelligence and vibrant personality willing to trust God even though her actions of faith might lead to her death—what does it mean for himself? Voices in the night giving page references in the Bible? What is going on? Yet he too is sensing a spiritual urgency in the air that he has never previously experienced.

The boys happily decamp at Peniel. For Tim it is his past home and anyway Mahmud and both the boys are close friends. They will have a good time. The servants are there to feed them. Bilquis brings some spare clothes. We don't know what kind of baptism to expect, sprinkling a la Presbyterian and Anglican or immersion a la Baptist. We will find out soon enough.

The drive up to Abbottabad into the mountains in wintertime is glorious. To the far distant northwest are the distant snow covered mountains of the Karakorums and the fields are green with the winter wheat. Bilquis reminisces about past journeys, not a bit nervous about her intended action and the possible reaction from those who love her.

Somehow in a remarkable way all the arrangements in Abbottabad have come together like pieces of a jigsaw puzzle falling through the air onto a table each into its perfect place. Everything is ready and waiting for us when we arrive. The baptism will be in the living room of a home. The curtains are drawn. The room is arranged as for a service. Some of David's friends are present as witnesses and congregation. Padri Bahadur will conduct the baptism. He is an ordained Presbyterian pastor who currently has no congregation and thus no session to consult for approval. He is working as a language teacher in Abbottabad.

Bilquis has been expecting a baptism by immersion, possibly in a river, lake or pond if a regular baptistry is not available but January is no time to try out the temperatures of the outside waters. Yes, Jesus had been immersed in the Jordan but that was 1,200 feet below sea level. Maybe, 4,000 feet up in the mountains in mid-winter, even John the Baptist might have resorted to sprinkling.

It is a simple and very moving ceremony. Padri Bahadur conducts it gravely and well. Synnove sings a hymn. There are a couple of different Bible readings. I read from Job. Padri Bahadur asks the questions of Bilquis and receives confident affirmative answers. He sprinkles her, declaring her baptized in the name of the Father, the Son and the Holy Spirit.

The unspoken background is the potential consequence to what is happening now when the baptism becomes known. We all know what *could* happen. Bilquis is perhaps the most composed of us all.

We sing a closing hymn. There is a benediction then congratulations and embraces for Bilquis from the women. We take only a short while for refreshments and head back home to the boys at Peniel.

On the way back, Bilquis lets us into a secret from this morning. She is already baptized! She has baptized herself. She has felt so constrained by the urgency to be baptized immediately that after we had seen the Mitchells and dropped her off she had Raisham fill her marble chip bathtub, raising the temperature with hot water from the hamam. She sat in the bathtub, placed her hand upon her own head and said, in a loud voice with no one to hear, "Bilquis, I baptize you in the name of the Father, the Son and the Holy Ghost." She pressed her hand down upon her own head and slid down in the tub until her whole body was totally immersed.

She spluttered up and out and dressed; relaxed and joyfully sure that come-what-may her baptism had been taken care of in the sight of her Father.

She has decided to tell us only on the return journey from Abbottabad lest there be some theological implications to what she has done of which she is not aware. As far as she is concerned she has been baptized both by immersion and by sprinkling on the same day. It feels good and one way or the other she has passed a milestone.

When we arrive back at Peniel we realize just how urgent has been the need for Bilquis to move quickly. Within an hour of our departure for Abbottabad the senior members of the family, uncles, cousins and aunts had come to the house in a body to see Bilquis and they had met only the servants and the three boys playing in the garden. The family, Nur Jan reports, had come to warn her about meeting with Christians.

Had Bilquis ignored them after having received their unanimous warning it would have been a serious affront to all who had been defied. Even as it is, how likely is it that the members of the family can overlook this defection by a senior family member from the faith of their fathers?

The Boycott

Bilquis is a member of a powerful and close-knit family. Its various branches are tied together by its long history and by the need in any family for unity. Unity means strength. In Eastern culture the family and its well-being has greater significance than individual well-being. You need each other and this is the kinship group that will close ranks around you if ever you are in trouble. The centuries have taught that you make little progress and you are highly vulnerable when you travel alone but when you travel as a group those who would do you harm hesitate. A corollary to this, an inverse, is that the individual lives out life within the limiting framework of the family's long-term interest and takes no actions to the detriment of the family group.

Bilquis has breached these unwritten rules. She has sought no consultation with the senior members of the family who love and respect her. She has given them no prior notice of her intended action. Her apostasy is detrimental to the family standing and deeply distressing to those who take their own faith seriously. Many of them do.

The first days after her baptism, Bilquis waits nervously for the family group to return to see her. We are much concerned for her and in touch daily. An aunt and then her uncle whom she loves greatly call and are left in no doubt of what has happened. She has no wish to hurt them but she is not going to try to deceive them. Much to Bilquis' relief, the whole group of family elders does not however return. Instead, a family meeting at the Big House decides that Bilquis will be completely boycotted.

Before this can take effect, Bilquis drives to Lahore to see Khalid, her only son. She has already talked to him over the phone and of course he has heard from various members of the family. They talk all afternoon. Khalid finds it hard to understand why it could not have been a personal and private action kept to herself and, perhaps, her children.

Tooni is more understanding. She lives close by in Pindi and works at the Holy Family Hospital. Over the past three months she has been observing the change in her mother. She is liking what she observes although she is disturbed by her mother's steadily increasing interest in reading the Bible. News of her mother's baptism is not welcome but does not really surprise her. Her concern enfolds not only her mother but also her son. Can Mahmud's father now reclaim custody of the child?

She comes out to see her mother with a couple of younger relatives. They talk freely. People, friends, are saying her mother will be murdered. Will Mahmud be allowed back into his mother's custody?

Mahmud, as well as Bilquis, now becomes for us a focus of our prayers. He is five years old and a delightful little boy. At the age of seven, or so Bilquis understands, his father will again have the right to determine his schooling and his custody. Will he elect to do so? Bilquis is never to be at ease over the one person she loves most in the entire world, her grandson, while she remains in Pakistan. She is learning the hard lesson that when you commit yourself totally into the arms of your loving heavenly Father, you have still to go one step further. You also have to commit the one or ones you love most in all the world to those same loving arms. Only then you can be at rest.

Friends, close personal friends, now come to see Bilquis at

Peniel. They also are afraid someone might kill her. The Q'ran on apostasy is clear. They urge her to keep her new faith secret, avoid publicity and she might survive. She explains why she cannot keep secret the public acknowledgment of her new faith. Yes, she understands that when trouble comes they will be unable to help her.

The boycott is now obvious. No one phones. No one calls, even to rebuke. When encountered in the street in Pindi or the lane in Wah, family all turn away or freeze their faces in disapproval. Family occasions, births, engagements and weddings are celebrated without her. Deaths are mourned without her. Only Marie and Tooni phone daily. Marie also writes a letter daily so that there will be something encouraging for Bilquis to look forward to in the mail.

Next, with the exception of Raisham, the Christian servants in the household, four of them, suddenly leave the servant quarters during the night and are gone. Have they been threatened or have they just decided to get out while it is still possible? Anonymous letters begin to arrive and there will be an occasional abusive phone call.

This is a learning time. Things are certain to get worse. Overriding all other concerns though Bilquis is convinced that nothing will or can happen unless her heavenly Father permits it. Therefore, whatever the gathering storm might bring it will only bring what He allows it to bring. Within that thought she can take courage. He will not forsake her even though the world and the heavens collapse about her ears.

Tooni

Taxila Hospital, February 1967

It is the thirteenth of February, evening. A fire is burning in the grate. We have had devotions after supper and the boys are back in their bedrooms playing with their toys or reading. Our guests are Paul and Clara Lindholm who are visiting Pakistan for a spell to assist the church in its understanding of stewardship. Suddenly our conversation is halted as an attractive young Pakistani woman, a stranger, bursts in, pauses, looks around at us, makes a choice and addresses me almost angrily. "Are you Ken Old?"

I nod and, rising, ask her to sit down and tell us why she has come. I am guessing she is Bilquis's daughter Tooni. Indeed, before she can begin to speak further, Bilquis herself comes in, smiles across at us and takes up her usual seat at the end of the settee. She is unusually quiet but quite composed and relaxed in herself. Neither the Lindholm's nor Bilquis say anything during our time together other than the pleasantries of greeting and farewell.

Marie delays going to get two more cups for our unheralded guests until she finds out why they have come.

"I'm Bilquis's daughter."

She unloads her heart without a pause for further introduction.

"I don't care whether my mother becomes a Christian, that's her business, but I don't want her to become a Christian martyr!"

"Why don't you tell us what has happened, Tooni?"

"What has happened! If you don't know you are the only people who don't know! Everybody else in Pindi and Islamabad knows it and I'd think you'd know it out here before them!"

Tooni sits herself down beside her mother. She is still angry but it has softened somewhat to a general angriness rather than anger personally directed against me.

"Yesterday the vicar of Christchurch in Pindi, Padri Waris, announced *from his pulpit* that the wife of General Sheikh, Begum Bilquis Sheikh, has become a Christian! He asked his entire congregation to be praying for my mother that she wouldn't be harmed. What are we, savages?"

I groan involuntarily. Who needs enemies when you have friends like this? It is easy to see what has happened. Padri Waris is an old acquaintance. We have known him since the orphanage days in Karachi. He is well intentioned but he can hardly have done a more unwise thing. The news has reached Tooni; she has called her mother who is in Pindi for a few days. To calm her down Bilquis has suggested to Tooni she go and see us at Taxila Hospital.

What on earth is this going to mean now? Fanatics exist in all cultures but you don't have to advertise victims. The family is going to be up in arms; the family name is being dragged through the mud. Bilquis has now been placed in jeopardy full in the public eye. It is an invitation for a reaction.

Bilquis's composure does not change; she is far more relaxed than her daughter.

I express my regrets at what has happened and try to reassure Tooni. "Tooni, one of two things can have happened to your mother. Let's think about them. The first is that she has made a horrible mistake, that her dreams and visions are fantasies, that Jesus is no more than a prophet and that what she has been believing all her life is still as true as it ever was. If that is what has happened then you can relax, you can even rejoice for your mother is a gentler sweeter woman now than she ever was before. You know that."

Tooni nods assent; she is listening carefully.

"Have no doubt, if this is all a mistake in belief, it will soon expose itself. You know your mother well enough to know she will never be content to live a lie. It will all be over in a few days and completely forgotten and your mother forgiven.

"But the other alternative is that what has happened to your mother is not fantasy but truth. Perhaps indeed your mother has met God, incredible as it may seem. You know from her own story that no missionaries, no Christians of any kind have had any hand in what has happened. This perhaps has been a simple one-to-One encounter between your mother and God.

"We and the Mitchells met your mother in December after this had happened to her in October and November. We have been as amazed as you are at what has happened and is happening.

"If, just if, this is indeed the case then you have even more reason to relax than if it were fantasy because she has fallen into the hands of a mighty God. He, for His own divine purposes, has a specific plan for your mother's life. We do not know what that is but we can be sure it is not with the intent that she should become a martyr. God, just because He is God, will completely cover your mother at all times and she will rest in His Shadow safer than she has ever been in her life.

"Tooni, if what has happened to your mother is true, and I am inclined to believe you feel it might be, then be at peace. We both believe in God and neither of us underestimates His power. I assure you of this. There is a phone in our house. If ever, at any time of the day or night, your mother phones us to say she is in trouble we will be at her house in twenty minutes. That is a promise and a commitment."

I do not add that her house is isolated, it is easy to cut telephone wires and calls can be intercepted at the exchange or blocked by the local operator. Tooni is as aware of that as I am.

I ask Tooni whether she has any objection to our praying together now for her mother's safety. She does not.

During a parting cup of tea, by now an empathy had been established, we assure Tooni that every day we will make sure we meet her mother, if she doesn't visit us we will go and see her. We will be checking on her every day.

Tears of Grief

February 28th, 1967

The significance of monthly dates is noticeable. On the 24th of
December Bilquis has sought and received the gift of the Holy
Spirit. On the 24th of January she has been baptized. Now the
significance changes to the 28th of the month. On three suc-
cessive 28ths of the month, an unexpected death occurs in the
village family.

First is a cousin who dies suddenly of a heart attack. His
mother's specific request that Bilquis be informed cannot be com-
plied with because of the strict boycott.

The custom of centuries when a death occurs is that acquain-
tances, relatives and friends go at the earliest possible moment to
share the grief of the nearest relatives by their silent sympathetic
presence. Mattresses, cushions or rugs are placed on the floors or
on the grass outside. Men sit in one area and women in another.
Few words are exchanged. The occasion is known as a *sorrowing*.
After a while sitting in silence or near silence the mourner will
quietly assure the closest relatives of sympathy and then resume
sitting for a while before leaving. It is a lovely and very moving
silent celebration of a sad occasion by the local community in
which enemies as well as friends participate.

Bilquis loved this cousin, he was near her own age and they
had played together as children. She feels strongly constrained

295

to breach the boycott against her from her own side by joining the sorrowing although she isn't looking forward to her inevitable rejection by the family. Her presence will undoubtedly be offensive to the others who are mourning and perhaps even to the nearest relatives.

Outside the cousin's home on the carpets and durries are the villagers sitting quietly. They are well aware of Bilquis' ostracism and watch her go into the house with silent surprise. Inside, members of the family, seeing her, turn their heads away. Among the women she sits quietly down. As she is observed, the low murmuring ceases. The traversing of beads between the fingers fumbles to a halt. One or two look at her then quickly look away. Bilquis lowers her eyes for her own prayers. She has come to *sorrow*, not to face and stare down a boycott. After a quarter of an hour the stilled murmur begins to pick up again. It is time to speak to her cousin's wife.

Quietly, observed by all, she walks over to the inner room where the open coffin rests until the burial in late afternoon before dark falls. Some of the closest family members are present, quietly verses of the Q'ran are being recited, the wife sits in a chair by the coffin and his mother kneels at its side. Bilquis goes over to the wife and quietly expresses her sorrow. "He has always been so kind to me and I too will miss him. May God give you comfort."

She looks at her dead cousin, now so pale and still and closes her eyes in silent prayer. On impulse she embraces the broken-hearted mother who looks up at her with tear-filled and grateful eyes. "I too loved him much, may God give you comfort."

As she walks back into the anteroom to take her place everything goes quiet again. A few cousins rise and shuffle out. This is clear rejection, not just an appropriate end to a visit. The quiet murmuring eventually resumes. Bilquis makes her brief farewells and goes to her car. Phew! That's a hurdle over. At least there has been no altercation.

On the 28th day of the following month again a death in the family occurs. Another male cousin, younger than the other, has died. Again Bilquis hears of his death through her servant's chatter.

This cousin has a five-year old, the same age as Mahmud. How tragic for the young widow and for that young child!

Again Bilquis feels strongly constrained to join the *sorrowing*. It is the same as before. This time Bilquis cannot help crying. Through her tears she approaches the widow beside the coffin, and finds to her surprise a hand stretched out toward her to greet her. This is the first sign of welcome she has received since her change of faith to acknowledge she even exists for the family. The two women embrace and for a few moments meet together in silent unity. "Thank you, Bilquis, thank you."

This time none of the cousins pointedly rise to leave as she returns to the anteroom.

On the 28th day of the third month, once again there is a sudden death and a funeral in the family. Once again the servants are the informants about what has happened. Once again Bilquis makes the journey down to the village. Once again she walks slowly through the seated sorrowing villagers. This time it is different inside. The family's solidarity is being shaken by these sudden deaths. All families have these occasions of bereavements close together but what is happening and why is it happening in this way?

Bilquis tells us with wonder in her voice that this third time it is as though the boycott has been temporarily lifted for the duration of the sorrowing. There is just too much accumulated grief to handle. Bilquis' tears are as acceptable and welcome as any others and the sympathy of her presence is valued. Her words of comfort are given from a genuinely loving and grieving heart. They are needed and accepted.

It is the beginning of the slow decay of the boycott.

A cousin's mother calls to thank Bilquis for her comfort and presence at her son's funeral. Another mother phones to thank her for comforting her son's widow. It will still take a year for all the hurriedly erected barriers to come down but slowly and surely the dismantling process takes place until it is all gone.

A Long Furlough

May 1967 – September 1968

At Christmas Marie and I met Bilquis and have grown to love her as a sister. When she realizes that we are going on furlough in May and we will be away for over a year, she can hardly bear the thought. She makes the seven-mile journey between her home at Wah Cottage and the Mission Hospital at Taxila almost daily, timing it for the ritual of morning tea. Marie is her confidante and counselor. They drink tea together and wait for me to come across to join them from the building site of the new operating block. We share new experiences we have had since we last met and pray together before I leave them to resume my work.

We reassure Bilquis that the Mitchells will be there for her even though visiting their home at the Cement Factory might attract more public attention than a visit to the hospital. We will write regularly. She will constantly be in our prayers. The time will pass quickly. God will be with her at all times.

The Sialkot Mission has a monthly newspaper that not only goes around to its missionaries on the field but also is circulated back home in the States to retired missionaries and others who are powerful in prayer for the Punjab. It is a lighthearted family newspaper with contributions from missionaries serving at each mission station there. The whole work is covered. There are discussions that are rarely theological, discussions about the chemistry of tea and lost washing machine motors. Marie for some years is editor of News Notes and writes a number of contributions:

March / April 1967: Marie Old, Taxila

The boys and Dr. Lall's son went off to school on the 7th (March) leaving the house very quiet. The next evening the Christy's arrived bag and baggage. They now seem to be all settled and both are at work.

With less than four hundred in-patients we can't say the eye season is in full swing but it is getting under way. With Norval and Dorothy to help, it should be a little easier for all of us this spring. Instead of the usual early morning operating schedule we now begin at 8 p.m. and finish anywhere up to 1 am. This is due to the fact that we only have electricity from 8 p.m. to 6 am – just when we don't need it most. This schedule does not mean that we don't start work again at 7:30 am – we do.

In February Kids Kamp was held here as usual with something like fifty kids (from Murree Christian School) to keep things lively. We understand that there were special blessings experienced by a number of the young people.

We have ourselves been greatly blessed this winter through the privilege of watching God work in two lives. Some of you will have heard of one through your children at camp. To watch God reveal Himself to her in a marvelous way has been a great joy and blessing to us. The other was a visitor from England who actually came seeking God, and who we feel has really found Him. Both have been a great encouragement to us at this the end of our term.

How often in life opportunities are created for us and yet we seem to just pass them by. I thought that moving from Sialkot to Taxila was such an opportunity. It would enable us to have that thorough spring cleaning and throwing away accumulated items and whatnot that previous removals had failed to accomplish. Unfortunately Ken moved while I was in Murree and so every empty bottle, every punctured bucket and every piece of bent pipe arrived here carefully packed and protected against harm.

When the Christys arrived here last week (they are very efficient and after two moves in a year are practically ready to take off for furlough at a moment's notice) I saw my chance. Ken had two desks in his office both so completely filled with tools; boxes of receipts, papers, paper clips and whatnot on top and inside that Norval's reclaiming of his desk presaged the inevitable. With nowhere else to put things we were in for a real cleanout.

For several days after the desk was removed Ken went through a traumatic experience wandering around like a lost soul: remaining out at work and using the excuse of no electricity not to work in the evenings. His desk was two feet high in litter and his drawing board even higher. Silently and sympathetically, I placed a few extra wastepaper baskets around his office and diplomatically made cheerful mention of my success in clearing out empty bottles and old books and talked about plans for our journey home.

I am sure Ken's reluctance to consider furlough plans is basically a reluctance to be separated from his rubber stamps, his checkbook stubs and his books on sewage treatment.

Anyway, his joy is now restored.

He still has his old brochures on closed circuit TV, his old ballpoint pens that won't write, his 1962 receipts and all his other clutter. He brought a door from his supplies and from it constructed a table. We have seen a miracle of rearrangement. Nine filing trays neatly filled. The contents of his drawers are now grotesquely on display on shelves where rubberstamps for missionaries long retired vie for visual attention with glass paperweights and old spectacles.

Not one wastepaper basket was filled. To encourage myself and Ken I added some of my junk to his baskets and there the matter rests.

Ken's system of packing the day before furlough may be all right for him but I know that when the day of retirement comes some years hence there will be those same empty bottles, old spectacles and unusable ball-point pens, etc.

Our new generator has come from England so, as soon as the wiring is ready, we will have our own electricity!

PS Urgent: Dr. Hamm has looked after many of you and your children during his two terms out here. Is there any among you who would be willing to care for his delightful little dog Tabby from say May 25 when we depart on furlough until the Hamms arrive in early June? This will be a fine way to repay Orval's many kindnesses to you and your family. Of course since our nice little dog Puff is also going to Orval he would be part of the bargain.

We are ready and waiting to hear from any of you.

At the end of May we leave on furlough. It has been an eventful term. There has been a war. Last summer we had moved back up to Taxila.

June and July we spend in England meeting and visiting with family we have not seen for five years. Then it is on to the States. There is no escaping responsibility this time for communicating mission to the home churches of our denomination in the Washington / Alaska area. We had done pretty well in the past in avoiding the denomination's headquarters, for since her return after Mac's death fourteen years previously Marie had only been back to the States once.

God provides a home for us in what is to become hereafter our American home base. Richland lies to the east of the Cascade Mountains in Washington State. It is close to the confluence of the Snake and Yakima Rivers with the Columbia River and lies within the V formed by the Yakima and Columbia. It is about 85 miles south of Marie's childhood home of Selah. The land had been desert. In 1942 a nuclear town was established there to process and provide the plutonium that would one day be used in a bomb dropped over Nagasaki in Japan.

West Side Church is a United Protestant Church with Presbyterian affiliation that caters for the needs of the west side of the town. We have met its remarkable pastor, Homer Goddard, as the zany dean of a Junior High kids camp in the mountains west of Selah when we were *missionaries in residence* during our previous furlough.

Homer and his family visit us in Pakistan shortly after the 1965 war. After a truck accident in the recently fought over area near Pasrur Isabelle sweetly turns to me as we come to a juddering halt with "There's no one I'd rather have had an accident with than you."

> *Time, you thief, who loves to put fruits into your list, put that in too.*

Now Homer and his family are transferring to Fresno in California. The church session requests us to come and live in the manse. If I will preach just one Sunday a month to give some continuity it will take care of the other Sundays and the church will not appoint an interim pastor for the period until a new pastor is called. They are taking a great risk. I am an engineer, not a preacher or pastor. However I do have a wonderful wife! A member of the church will make a car available. The school the boys will attend is a close walk away.

I have a speaking engagement in a Denver church in late August. Marie and the boys will fly from London direct to Seattle over the Arctic. I will go ahead via New York and Denver to Richland, pick up the car and meet them at the SeaTac airport.

God uses many different ways to communicate with people. He speaks during prayer time or while studying Scripture. Sometimes He uses audible voices; other times the message comes through an *inner* voice. He communicates through dreams and visions, even *time-jumps* and premonitions. He will also reveal himself through books and conversations. Inner *certainties* fixed on the mind or wise counsel of others can be God making Himself known. An event, or a series of events, and *coincidences* that are not coincidences become tools used by God to communicate with us. And He sometimes speaks through sermons.

Between New York and Denver it becomes clear to me that a particular phase of our lives is about to come to an end. Something new, somewhere, is about to happen to us. It will not be a matter of our exercising choices but allowing a series of events planned somewhere beyond us to happen.

On Sunday in New York I go to church, probably Riverside Church on Morningside Heights. The text for the sermon is a verse in Revelation 3:8–*"Behold, I have set before thee an open door."* That is a verse I have never particularly noted before.

On Monday morning before heading for the airport my devotional reading for the day is a meditation on the same passage. Curious.

The magazine I read on the plane opens at an article where the writer exposits on the meaning of the message in Revelation to the church in Philadelphia, particularly the meaning and significance of the passage *"Behold, I have set before thee an open door."*

More curious.

By the time I reach Denver I have accepted that God is trying to tell me something and it is probably something I don't want to hear.

At this time I am a rather ordinary civil engineer married to an extraordinary American missionary nurse and I have no career change in view. I'm content with what I am doing. I am involved in designing and then building an operating theater block in an amazing village hospital in Pakistan and I'm not even half way through. It could take at least a further two years after we return from furlough. After that there will be other building work, my particular assignment is as the mission builder and there is always a backlog of work waiting to be tackled.

If there are changes to the pipeline I'm not anxious to hear about them.

Marie picks up her assignment as Editor of News Notes when we return to the hospital at Taxila the following year:

September 1968: Marie Old, Taxila:

As usual this time of year Taxila is pretty busy. There are about seven hundred in-patients, which keeps everyone from sitting around too much.
Before we were unpacked or settled we had the first of what will, we hope, be a long list of visitors from our home

church in America. They were Lane and Gwen Bray who had been to a conference in Haifa where Lane delivered a scientific paper. They had a good introduction to the East when they discovered in Kabul that the Afghan Airline just wasn't having its scheduled flight the day they were to come to Rawalpindi. They took a taxi and enjoyed the ride through the Khyber Pass in spite of the fact they had nothing to eat all day.

I came home from seeing the boys in Murree on Sunday to find our house full of young English world travelers. Six of them had crawled out of a VW which had rolled over a few times just in front of Bilquis Sheikh's house. Bilquis took them in, gave them tea, calmed them and then brought them to Ken. This is Friday and they are still here, some staying with Bilquis and some with us. Their problem is what to do with the car. Their recommendation is that if you are traveling in Pakistan on a carnet don't have an accident. The Government has said they have to pay 20,000 rupees duty OR take the car out of the country. Since it is a heap of wreckage the latter is impossible. The former is also impossible since they don't have twenty thousand rupees. One embassy official suggested they truck it to Karachi and dump it in the ocean. The British High Commission is coming out today to advise them and they hope to be on their way by Monday.

They have been very helpful, at least the ones at our house have. They got our truck off blocks and onto the road for Ken, fixed my washing machine and electric oven and have done just lots of odd jobs.

They are not the usual world travelers. They even put on suits and ties for dinner in the proper British tradition. They have been amazed at Bilquis's story and witness and *the ones with us say that their lives will never be the same again. They are thinking perhaps God has a plan for their lives also.*

Dorothy Christy and the children arrived from furlough about the middle of June. Norval came the first week of July and we arrived on September 5th.

Our furlough was not exactly an uneventful one. Ken had an interpretation assignment with the Synod of Washington / Alaska and that is a considerable piece of territory to cover, so the boys and I saw very little of him. We did go with him to Point Barrow, Alaska which is the most northerly point on the American continent and three hundred miles inside the Arctic Circle. It was cold enough, about fifty or sixty degrees below freezing with ice and snow everywhere. We found a most fascinating church in that ice and snowbound town, one that has about 100 out to prayer meeting regularly and between 200–300 on Sundays. We had a packed church for nearly a week of meetings. The boys thought it was all wonderful and enjoyed caribou stew in an Eskimo home and raced over the snow on skidoos.

The furlough, beginning in May a year previously, has been partially spent helping to cover the gap in Richland, Washington, left by the pastor's departure. We live in the manse of the church. It has given our two boys their only opportunity for schooling outside Pakistan in an American school. While I travel around speaking in churches, Marie spends her time creating a home for and caring for the boys. She makes many close and enduring friendships within the West Side Church community. Her correspondence routine never flags. The letters are largely sent back to her Pakistani friends, Bilquis primary among them.

We have enjoyed the furlough but we are all glad to be home again and Bilquis, of course, is delighted we are back.

Bilquis Goes Abroad

September 1968

In September of 1968 I am able to resume the construction of the operating block at Taxila Hospital. Bilquis is holding on strongly, the Mitchells have been making sure she has had good fellowship and encouragement while we were away. She is attracting visitors; some are Muslims, even newly converted Muslims, who wish to persuade her to revert to her old beliefs. Others are Christians from other countries who have heard of her conversion. One of them, Dr. Stanley Mooneyham of World Vision, based in California, invites her to participate in a congress in Singapore arranged by Billy Graham *Christ Seeks Asia*.

The day after her arrival she speaks, and speaks well and clearly, to thousands upon thousands of people gathered in the rising galleries of a great auditorium. This is her first experience of a multitude of very genuine rejoicing Christians and she is uplifted by it. She meets at this conference Christy Wilson of Kabul.

If I recollect correctly, Bilquis tells me she is accosted and threatened with violence by several Muslim men either in the corridor of her Singapore hotel just outside her room or else by intruders into her room. The organizers of the conference take the incident seriously. They decide a further engagement in another country is unwise and that she should return to Pakistan without delay for her own safety. This she does.

After furlough we pick up again our friendship and our visits. Bible studies at Peniel resume and we continue to be surprised at the Christian maturity that this woman has achieved in such a short time. We are frequently learning from her even though I am leading the studies.

In October 1970 this is all to end for we leave Taxila to work in Gujranwala about one hundred and seventy miles away towards Lahore. Bilquis as a Christian is nearly three years old. Marie and Bilquis remain in close touch by letter. Whenever an opportunity presents itself we visit each other.

An attempt is made to set fire to Peniel in 1971. Bilquis feels suddenly constrained to rush outside with Mahmud in haste and discovers blazing wood set against the side of the house. It is only just brought under control.

A political change at the end of 1971 brings about the rise of a new political party, the People's Party, and a radical social-ist form of government. Expropriation of properties from the landed families threaten the wealth of Bilquis and members of her Wah family.

Bilquis, in July 1972, drives with Tooni and Mahmud to Lahore for a short visit to see Khalid and to arrange for the sale of some of the family properties before they are taken. Although she does not know it, she is not to return for many years. Warnings have been coming to Bilquis in recent months that attempts are to be made on her life. Some seem ominously likely; solid plans rather than products of the rumor mill. She is now paying seri-ous attention to them and is nervous for what might happen to Mahmud if plans succeed.

Now we begin to observe, in a few short days, the concurrences of God—Madame Guyon's *"all things conspire to one great end."*

Bilquis phones Marie from Khalid's. She is in our area; can we meet? We won't be able to get to Lahore for a few days to see her but Marie phones Peggy Schlorholz, a missionary friend resident at Forman Christian College and asks her to make contact. That is a critical connection. Peg is on the phone to Bilquis in a few moments. This leads to Peg going to Khalid's, hearing Bilquis' story first hand and bursting out, "Oh I wish you could come to the United States with me!" Peg is leaving soon for a four-month furlough to put her son in school and would love to have Bilquis speak in the churches she is planning to visit. It is Peg who is to facilitate the writing and publication of Bilquis' story and be instrumental in the subsequent phase of Bilquis' life.

Bilquis, visiting Peg several days later on a return visit, mentions she has met a Dr. Christy Wilson of Kabul while in Singapore. Does Peg know where he is? The phone rings as they speak. Perhaps no surprise, it is Christy Wilson visiting Lahore entirely unexpected from Afghanistan. He is coming out for a visit. Christy hears of Peg's spur-of-the-moment dream to take Bilquis to the States. He strokes his chin and wonders whether he might not know someone who would like to help. Within just a few days, full sponsorship has been arranged and confirmed for all travel expenses for both Bilquis and Mahmud.

There are seven days now to make all arrangements, without access to all her clothes and possessions back in Wah. Her personal treasures and photographs she will have to leave behind. Visas will be needed but oho!—the passports, revalidated for Singapore, are in the drawer of a bureau in Peniel. Dare she hasten back to get them? That would be dangerous and unwise!

Marie and I come from Gujranwala on a shopping trip and call in to see Peg. Bilquis is there. Happy reunions! Maybe we can help. Within two days I am back from Wah village with the passports. The visas prove no problem. Three days remain; only the Income Tax Clearance needs to be obtained.

This is always the windup activity before leaving the country.

The government wishes to know you have paid all the taxes you owe it before you will be allowed to leave. Bilquis and Khalid head for the large circular building on Naba Road.

Something strikes them as odd immediately they enter the building. Outside everything is normal but inside is silence. Where are the people? A single clerk reading a newspaper is located. He looks up. "There's a strike on!" Ouch, what now? So close, why this block? "When does the strike end?" The clerk spreads his hands in a gesture of ignorance. "Who knows, it is an indefinite strike."

Bilquis has had many dealings with government offices before; her father was a government minister. She knows that even when underlings strike the superiors turn up for work and sit in their offices reading newspapers to avoid being tarred with the strikers' brush. She asks to see the person in charge.

Sure enough, there is one. They sit before him. He has no underlings to run to his orders but he will listen. "What is your problem, Begumsahiba?"

Bilquis begins. First she gives her name. Recognizable names carry great weight in a country of influence and prestige. If you have a known name, don't hesitate to use it. The officer puts up his hand as she proceeds. His face is animated and curious. "Begum Sheikh? Are you the begum of General Sheikh? Oh, the Simple Living Plan, that was your work, was it not? A pity it didn't go even further. What can I do for you?"

Problems, even difficult problems, have a way of evaporating when confronted by a resolute will. This officer has one. There is in the building one new employee who has not yet joined the union. He types out the certificate. The officer himself applies the rubber stamp, signs with a flourish and the job is done.

Bilquis and Mahmud are on their way to a Christian country. What will they find there?

Calm Waters

Peg Schlorholz is a wonderful guide to this uprooted woman and her grandson from Pakistan. They have only the few unplanned possessions they have brought with them and little prospect of return to their own dearly beloved country. They need help.

They will have to choose a place to live, settle and create roots and somehow survive. Assets that Bilquis has in Pakistan are not transferable and will be little use to her in a new country.

Bilquis has come to the United States expecting to see the country of her recent dreams. This is a country of mystical cities that she has mentally associated with the United States. They are cities filled with churches, skylines of towers and steeples reaching heavenwards. She is finding to her surprise that some of those dreamed about scenes are indeed recognizable. There are many churches in the cities but worryingly the crowds in the Sunday streets seem more bound for recreation than church. How can this be when there is nothing to be afraid of and they can worship freely? Do they not understand Jesus has died for them?

Bilquis is to learn fast. She has a gift of astute perception and comes from a background that gives a detached view of money. She sees beneath the hoopla of effervescent Christianity and shares in her letters to us her disillusion with the commercialization of Christianity. She is on her guard against becoming a puppet or a pawn in the hands of religious circus operators. Christianity is becoming, perhaps has already become, show business.

Her Christ has not died for a reward of spotlights and tinsel. She is usually able to sort the sincere from the spurious quickly and accurately but she picks her steps carefully.

Somehow she has at any cost to retain the reality she knows. She has to have silence and quietness. She has to hold on to the sweet communion with her Lord that means more than anything. She has learned how to recover it when she loses it in Peniel—go back to the last time she has felt the closeness of His presence and then search the trail for the point of divergence where she has lost contact with Him. Then pray herself back into fellowship and not give up praying until it happens.

She is for a while in the Chicago area and then settles in La Crescenta, California. Mahmud has to go to school. She decides that, for safety's sake, he shall have a new name and allows him to choose both first and last names. David and Goliath is his favorite Bible story and so David as a first name is easy. The last name is also easy—he likes going on holiday more than anything so his second name will be Holiday.

Bilquis senses she is being followed. When she happens to turn suddenly around to look at Mahmud skipping along behind her a head ducks out of sight behind a parked car. When she goes for a walk a man on a street bench studies her from behind a newspaper. Is she imagining things? This is America after all, not Wah village. Several times she moves to a different house. She is seeing the same men in the streets. She *is* being watched, she is certain of it. Who are they after, her or Mahmud?

There is a failed attempt to kidnap Mahmud. The police are quick and a man is apprehended. A city judge now has to deal with Mahmud's father who has come to the States to try to recover his oldest son. The magistrate takes the boy into his chambers and privately asks him whether he wishes to return to Pakistan with his father or remain with his grandmother. Mahmud has no hesitation. The judge passes an order that leads to the father returning immediately, empty handed, to Pakistan.

God provides for Bilquis a woman, an unmarried American woman, who feels clearly led to be Bilquis' aide, assistant, secretary, helper and general factotum. Thus for a number of years she is a valuable associate.

When we visit Bilquis in Thousand Oaks, California, where she finally settles, we discuss her desire to return home. We strongly advise against either of the pair returning to Pakistan. Probably no one will harm her but it would be easy for someone to level criminal cases against her in a dozen different courts and trap her forever in a cycle of litigation. Defendants facing criminal charges aren't allowed to leave the country without permission of the courts. Perhaps when Mahmud reaches manhood and if he has acquired U.S. nationality it might be safe for him to go back, it probably will never be safe for Bilquis.

In this new world Bilquis is steadily acquiring influential Christian friends. They recognize in this Asian woman the rare quality of her spiritual experiences. A childlike trust and a mature mind bringing together a striking adventure into spiritual unknowns in an inimical setting that requires courage and steadfastness. They urge her to put the story of her discovery of a loving Father God into writing. She has her journal with her—that can provide the support to her memory that she will need. Dick Schneider in Virginia provides the professional assistance she needs. In 1978 *I Dared to Call Him Father* is published.

The remainder of Bilquis' story borders almost on fantasy and will not be told at length here. Mahmud studies to become a dental surgeon at Oral Roberts University in Tulsa, Oklahoma. He returns to Pakistan for a visit. His father dies while he is there. He inherits his father's estates and becomes a Member of the National Assembly of Pakistan. Bilquis returns to her beloved country and manages Mahmud's estates while he is in Islamabad recovering them from gross mismanagement.

In 1997 at Easter time, six months before Marie's death, Bilquis dies in Rawalpindi. She has had heart surgery and that might have been a contributory factor. She remains an unwavering Christian to the end of her life. Appropriately David Mitchell who was present at the beginning of her Christian life officiates at her funeral service. All her family are in attendance.

She lies buried in the little British army cemetery in Murree, six thousand feet up in the hills beyond Islamabad. She had given her friend, the President of Pakistan, a Bible while in Islamabad. Murree is one of her favorite little hill towns. From it you can look towards Pindi and then beyond, swinging your eye clockwise, to the Margalla hills. In them, northwest, rises the Dhamra River which flows past her door. Over the hills is the Christian hospital, Taxila, the Wah plain, Wah village and, on the outskirts, a lonely white cottage. Does the name Peniel still remain, I wonder.

> *Jacob called the place Peniel*
> *'because' he said,*
> *'I have seen God face to face*
> *and my life is spared.'*
>
> *—Genesis 32:30*

September 1999. A letter from a friend in Islamabad, Pakistan:

> *Bilquis' grandson Mahmud was killed in a tragic way this last Friday night. A heated discussion took place at his home some miles outside of Islamabad in which he was trying to mediate between his cook and the family of*

the girl his cook had abducted. One of her brothers struck Mahmud twice with an axe on the shoulder and neck and he died en route to the hospital.

An English Home

January 1973

During 1970, in the autumn, we transfer from Taxila to the city of
Gujranwala in the heart of the Punjab. We do not want to go but
I have been appointed to be Principal of the Technical Training
Centre there. It will be in Gujranwala that we are going to spend
the next twenty years of our lives. Marie is even more reluctant to
leave Taxila than I.

In 1972 we are recognizing that before long, at the most two
years, our lives will have to radically change. The boys will then

be seventeen and will need to leave home and return to England for further schooling or for training and work. Marie particularly is also realizing that neither Colin nor Tim is equipped for that alien culture and wondering what that will mean, not only for them but also for her.

It is true that since the end of the war in 1945 the nature of missionary service has radically changed. Advances in personal travel, the plane replacing the ship, mean that few families now serve five to seven years before returning to their homeland. Advances in communication mean that letters to and from home are delivered in a week rather than a month or longer. The telephone is a normal instant way of keeping abreast of family and friends half a world away. Advances in medicine mean that the missionary cemeteries in many lands have few recent additions and it becomes normal for patients to fly back home for treatment or consultation.

There is now for many missionaries very little sacrifice in missionary life except perhaps that of personal privacy, separation from children and, as Stephen Neill says, "*we become aliens in our own countries.*"

I doubt that the latter is in fact a sacrifice; for the greater compensation surely is that we become citizens of another country and willing captives to a fresh culture.

Many countries that receive missionaries make here, I believe, an error of understanding. They do not want missionaries because the indigenous faiths are threatened or feel threatened by proselytizing Christianity.

On the other hand, however, these newcomers are people who commit to that new land wholeheartedly. They study its language or languages and become fluent. They seek to understand its culture. They understand its politics. They understand the *way* people think and thus why they think and act as they do.

They empathize with its needs and are concerned for its poor and underprivileged. They are activists for good and uninterested in opportunities for exploitation. Many of their concerns are medical, social or educational and they often have much to offer. This new land becomes home to them, they adopt its dress and they are happiest when they are there.

Inevitably and very significantly they become articulate and well informed ambassadors for their adopted countries. They have keenly interested audiences in their own countries, for they have high credibility.

Wisdom suggests that developing countries with an image problem should open their doors wider and wider to long-term missionaries rather than seeking to keep them as closed as possible.

I write to Tony, my brother. He lives in England some thirty miles from Canterbury and, being a builder by trade, sees much of the countryside. The two boys are English, had they been American we might have looked for a home base in the States but this does not occur to us. Throughout her life Marie retains her American nationality but she is happy to find a home in England even though nagging at her mind is the thought that she might need to spend time away from Pakistan.

Tony reports back promptly. There is little likelihood of finding an inexpensive cottage within a few miles of Canterbury as we have asked. House prices have soared. He himself has been searching for his own family and has gone as far afield as East Anglia and Cornwall without finding a suitable property that he can afford. We should wait until we come home and look around for ourselves. It will not be easy and we should be prepared for disappointment.

The matter of where the boys might live is becoming urgent. It will not be fair to foist them upon their grandparents although they would undoubtedly be willing. They are our responsibility and not theirs.

Colin is likely to graduate first, in June 1974. That will be the time of our long furlough 1974 / 75 when we will be expected to do deputation work in the United States; our previous furlough had been 1967 / 68. We better go to England during the boys' winter holiday from Murree this coming December. This will give us three months to look for a house before we have to return them to school in early March.

On arrival in England the very first matter is to become mobile. At the Medway Car Auction in Maidstone I bid forty pounds for a Morris car and understandably, in view of its condition, it is the top bid.

One of its detractions that has deterred other buyers is that somehow over the many years of its life the windshield has become heavily scratched. These days we could assume that it had been parked in a Zoo park and a pride of lions had used it for years for filing their claws. Before the era of zoo parks, a suitable explanation fails unless we entertain the idea of glass-scratching mice. Now this is not as serious an impediment as it sounds. Only after dark does it become a problem. During daylight it is possible to squint between the scratches and navigate unerringly. After dark you are driving head-on into a battery of searchlights alternating with total darkness. The scratches refract every ray of light they can seize hold of and break them into a thousand golden pieces. Marie would just close her eyes if we should be out after dark. I presumed she was praying.

The remedy is actually quite simple—get off the road before dark! This means, in mid winter, very short days for exploration and, of course, occasionally we don't quite make it.

It does not take long as we drive around in those short hours to recognize the truth of Tony's remarks. It is going to be difficult to find a place. We might need to search again when we come home in 1974.

As soon as Christmas is over we get down more seriously to searching.

Two of our close missionary friends are Len and Audrey Adams. They have been in the Afghan Border Crusade stationed in Kohat in northern Waziristan where Marie and Mac had once been designated to serve. Marie had been their first missionary acquaintance when they arrived in Pakistan in 1950. One of their children had died there of smallpox. They have stayed with us when two of their children are born. After they had come home in 1961, they had been deeply disappointed not to be able to return to Pakistan.

Len gives us careful directions how to find where they are living. It is fifteen miles south of Canterbury. It will be difficult to find. Once in Sellindge, reputedly the longest village in Kent, find Brook Lane off Swan Lane and head across the common to the large white house standing on its own on the other side.

We share our concern about a house with Len and Audrey. They are equally unhopeful. They know of nothing. During later conversation after lunch, one of them mentions the farm next door. A well-known actress had been interested at one time to buy it, it is now derelict, has been so for some years.

Our afternoon walk on the common discovers the gate of the farm fronting onto the common. To say the farm is both desolate and derelict is almost an understatement. Beyond the gate, well behind the barbed wire fence, the field of brambles, thorns and tall weeds turned brown, are the remnants of a few abandoned farm buildings. There is a stone walled slate roofed barn; a cattle shed, also of stone, and a half-timbered farmhouse roofed with traditional Kentpeg tiles. All the roofs have holes in them. The farmhouse roof looks as though it has been deliberately vandalized. The wattle and daub walling upstairs has a hole the size of a door in it. Abandoned farm machinery is half buried by weeds. The five barred steel gate is chained close but even that cannot keep people out. A despairing sign says simply *"Trespassers will be prosecuted. J. Davies, Edenbridge."* Not even a telephone number or an address, just a town thirty-five miles away.

As we walk up the overgrown path, the property looks worse the nearer we get. The transepts of the barn are wide open, filled with hay, gathered or blown over years there is little telling. There are openings in the walls but no windows or doors. The cowshed has holes in the roof and stone walls and the stables; the third side of a partial rectangle has a corrugated sheet roof, one open gable end and a pair of door openings.

The house itself is in the worst condition of all. It is as though a team of hobgoblins has blown through it at Michaelmas, deliberately destroying with elemental violence everything that is portable or remotely fragile. The building has obviously two parts, one probably early Tudor and the other Georgian. The Georgian front door hangs on one hinge, half open. Other doors are nailed shut. The window openings are blocked with corrugated sheet and nailed up doors. Inside, a wrecked piano teeters on the broken floor joists into the water cellar, a staircase no longer usable struggles upstairs from the hall and, around the corner, a tiny twisting second staircase also leads upstairs. In the Tudor section, a hand-pump still survives in the earthen floor but does not work. There are no toilets but a small privy beyond the open well in the garden.

There are unkempt fields around the property of two or three acres.

It is all very isolated, and intriguing.

I am entranced, Marie less so. I copy what is written on the warning sign and stuff the paper in my pocket.

Gibbins Brook Farm

February 7, 1973

It promises to be a busy day. At 8 o'clock Marie is due at Bromley General Hospital to have some fatty tumors removed from her left arm. Over the years she has had a number removed and they have proved benign. However her recent breast cancer and mastectomy has made us very alert. This visit to England is an opportunity to get the tumors excised. We also have an appointment in Mayfair at 10 a.m. with a property owner. It will be a little tight on time but hopefully we will make it.

When returning to Sidcup from Sellindge after that first visit I talk to Tony. He is working in Islington and staying in London each night. When he phones home that evening Mary, his wife, asks him to call us.

The call is to change his life and that of his family.

I have seen a property which I might be able to buy. I tell him where the property is. IF this property is available for sale and we can afford to buy it then would he be interested to buy a portion of the property for himself, paying for it with his own labor? I know he has very little money but this might be an opportunity for him to obtain his own property. As further money becomes available to me, I will let him have it to buy building materials for the farmhouse. When his debt of labor is paid I will pay him for any further work he does on the house. We can only do this if he thinks he can get the house into living condition by next year, the summer of 1974.

We agree to meet at Sellindge the following morning at 10:30.

Audrey serves us tea and again we walk through the common over to the farm. Marie expects Tony to break into laughter at the absurdity of trying to repair this relic and shrugs with hopelessness. Tony however stays silent. He is taking everything in. My thought is that he will have the barn and the cowshed and we will have the house and the stables for a garage. He will be able to build further as he needs later. We explore everything that is accessible. There is active woodworm in the oak of the farmhouse. There will need to be a complete self-contained sewage system and the water supply is dependent on one small well. There is water in the well.

Tony is a master builder. Almost all the building trades are at his fingertips, from cabinetmaker to bricklayer to plasterer to plumber and pipe fitter, roofer and tiler. He is a passable electrician. He is thinking carefully. He has children with schooling to consider. His wife is from a London suburb, not a rural background. Inevitably the first years will be very rough. He will need help; one pair of hands can't do it all.

"It's possible," he says, "it's possible but it will take a lot of work and I don't know how Mary will feel about it."

Marie asks him how much he thinks the property is worth in its present condition. "Not more than £27,000, most of the cost is going to be in making it habitable. I don't think you should pay more than that. But if you can get it, yes, I'm with you and even if I can't get it fully ready I'll have it ready to live in by next summer."

On returning to Sidcup from Sellindge this second time, I write a brief letter to the mysterious Mr. Davies at Edenbridge. The address is inadequate but there is just a chance that it might be delivered. I have seen the property at Gibbins Brook Farm and would like to hear from him if he is interested in selling it.

We receive a phone call. It isn't the Mr. Davies from Edenbridge but the secretary of the owner of the property, phoning from an address in Mayfair in the West End of London. The letter has been forwarded. "Is this a serious inquiry?" "Yes, it is." We arrange to meet at 10 a.m. on February 7th.

As we are about to leave the house for Bromley on our way to the appointment, I realize that possibly we will be faced with making a decision about the purchase of the farm and although we have been praying we have had no clear guidance yet.

Probably the most widely used of all devotional books by Christians other than the Bible is Daily Light, simply a morning and evening collection of Bible verses.

During some early years of the 19th century, the Rev Bagster used to keep his family busy around the meal table by giving them a verse he had chosen for the day. The children and any others kenneth g. old

present would then nominate other verses that had a bearing on the lead verse. Those verses were collected into 732 different sets and they form the morning and evening readings for each day of the year.

I suddenly remember we have not read Daily Light for today. Although we search frantically as we are about to leave, we cannot find the book. We will have to go without referring to it. Marie settles herself into the car, it is 7:30 and time is running. I begin to reverse out of the drive and Marie cries "Here it is!" I stop as Marie removes Daily Light from the glove compartment. "What does it say, what does it say?"

It has become very important to know what guidance Daily Light has for us.

Marie reads slowly, the lead verse was from Deuteronomy 8,

When thou hast eaten and are full . . . thou shalt bless the Lord thy God for the good land which he hath given thee.

"He means us to have it" I burst out. "He means us to have it!" and I know, we know, that God intends us to have Gibbins Brook Farm as our home and that His Hand is in it.

Marie's tumors have been removed; several patches decorate her left arm. We are caught up now in the developing rush hour as we thread our way through Lewisham and New Cross and onto the Old Kent Road. The traffic is getting heavier. Marie asks how much I think we could, should, pay for the farm if it is indeed available.

"It's worth at least £20,000," I answer, "and I think the bank will lend us the money until we can transfer our savings from the States."

Marie's retort is prompt and firm. "We can't afford that, £15,000 is the most we can afford."

This is Marie's natural caution at work dealing with my optimism. She has had much practice at it. I think she would have taken 75% of any figure I happened to suggest. My response is that while I talk with the owner of the property, she sits at the back of the room and prays.

The traffic grinds to a halt. There is little sign of movement. Both directions of traffic are stalled. The minutes tick away. I am doing calculations mentally on the time it will take to get to Mayfair when suddenly we are enveloped in a cloud of steam splendidly erupting from under the hood of the Morris like a mini-Vesuvius.

I would have said that the Morris has shown better than average reliability. That would mean that the car completes its journey on average more than once in every two journeys, but probably not by a large amount.

Have you ever wondered whether Guardian Angels get frustrated? I am sure there must be times in the experience of such heavenly creatures when they feel like stamping their feet at some particularly inane action by their earthly charge or charges. Their antennae (if they have antennae) must go into mega-vibrations to try to cope with the fallout from ill considered actions—such as buying a car for £40 and then taking it up the Old Kent Road in the rush hour towards an urgent appointment the other side of the Thames when only rust secures the radiator against leakage.

In this case my G.A. performs superlatively.

When all the traffic ahead has eventually cleared and nothing behind is able to move, the driver of the truck right behind jumps out and joins me in pushing Marie, an embarrassed substitute driver, along and up a side road where the car can be abandoned. The Pakistani greengrocer at the corner shop is delighted to respond to my request in Urdu to keep an eye on the car until we can get back to collect it. After all, "We are brothers!"

It is now after 9:30. I knock on the side window of a car in the stalled traffic. There is only the driver and he rolls down the window. "Excuse me, we have had a breakdown and we need to pick up a taxi. Can you please give us a lift until we find one?" The driver, as we filter along through traffic jams, proves to have come from little more than a hundred yards from where we ourselves started out this morning. Not only that, he is going to the same address in Mayfair that we are heading for! Thank you, G.A.

At 10 a.m. on the dot he drops us at the door of our destination and goes off to park his car. We don't see him again but hurry up the several flights of stairs to the office. The secretary is charming, the property owner curious. He had bought the property as a country cottage for use at weekends but his wife has made it an *either / or* issue—*either* our marriage *or* the cottage, you can't have both. He has tried to get repairs done but the local children have destroyed in the evenings what the workmen have accomplished during the day. What makes us think we can do any better?

We explain our circumstances. We are missionaries. Our sons have to come home from Pakistan next year and we have to provide a home for them. My brother will live on the site and protect the work from vandalism.

We are seriously interested to buy, what will it cost? "I'll sell it to you" he says generously (after all these poor people must be crazy anyway), "for the price it cost me together with all the financing charges since. How does that sound? I'll have my secretary check what that will be."

It takes only a few moments for the amount to be produced—£13,300.

Marie, sitting quietly at the back of the room, lets out a breath. I am unsure whether it is dismay, joy or just a relief of tension. We agree, shake hands, exchange the names of our solicitors and leave to catch a train home and arrange for the recovery of the Morris.

The story of Gibbins Brook Farm is a romance in itself still to be told. Over thirty years of Tony's life have been spent in loving this beautiful old place back into life. A recent surveyor valued the property at £600,000 but it is not for sale. It is a stewardship we have been given.

Within a week I have an emergency call from Gujranwala to get back immediately. I am back in Pakistan by the 16th of February. It is left to Marie to wind things up in England and find a new owner for, or otherwise dispose of, the Morris.

If the appointment in Mayfair had been just a few days later it could never have happened!

Letter from Marie

Gujranwala

Life goes at such a pace I can't keep up!

The boys have been home from school since Friday and life is settling down to its new way with them here. Colin is working in the drawing office helping Ken with drawings for a new hostel just now. Tim will be spending his time doing I'm not sure what. I hope he will do a good bit of practicing on the piano and we will go to Lahore twice a week to play the organ at the Cathedral if we can manage the proper permissions. It is a long drive, ninety miles round trip, but we will have to do it.

Ken is so busy he almost doesn't even eat with us unless we drag him from the office. The housing project has become a very tremendous thing and takes all his time. He has almost turned the school over to the vice principal now. The Prime Minister's assistant frequently calls him about the housing and he is planning a village for him in Sindh.

We have a delightful guest from England, a violinist about thirty years old who has been here once before. He is now in Nepal but should be back this week. The boys are

333

anxious for him to come home. He teaches violin and viola in schools in England. We enjoy having him so much.

When this letter is finished I'll be preparing tea for a few of the staff who will be coming over to talk about the school Christmas program. These are the young single staff. They usually have lots of ideas.

I wish you could see our poinsettias – a whole hedge of them at the end of the lawn so beautiful after the rain. The blossoms are the size of dinner plates and the plants are about ten feet tall. The chrysanthemums are gorgeous just now too, the loveliest we have ever had. I am sitting on the screened verandah as I write and it is like a florist's shop.

This is our boys' last winter here. They go back to school in March for the last time.

Tim is just playing the Hungarian Rhapsody, number something. He can do very well if he wants to. His trouble is that he plays by ear and is really now trying to do it by reading the notes and it is hard.

Marie

Marie's Flexible Family

Marie runs a household of irregular size.

Our boys never know, when they come down from boarding school, what kind of ménage they are rejoining for the winter. They are only home three months in the year. They are always eager to get back to their dogs, their Pakistani friends and the activity and interaction of a house that is never boring.

It is hard to know from meal to meal how many extra sections will need to be inserted in the table. The boys become accustomed to Mom calling them into the kitchen just before a meal for an admonition to "Go easy on the meat" or, much worse, "Go easy on the potatoes." Some of the guests are Pakistanis but mostly they are foreigners. Visitors passing through know they can drop in and meet a generous smile, receive an invitation to a meal and, if they need it, an overnight stay and an opportunity for a refreshing bath.

Many of the extra bodies around the table will be youngsters in their late teens and early twenties. We have an immense admiration for them. Most of them have been young men. Marie loves it though when God gives her daughters for a while. Two of her nieces who come to help Uncle Ken develop an unusually close bond with her and count this unforgettable experience one of the most valuable in their lives.

Some of these youngsters have come out specifically to work with us and have been sponsored by churches and missionary societies at home or by their parents. Some have been referred to us by other missionaries who have less capacity to absorb willing workers who are without command of the language.

Some just arrive on the doorstep. Marie considers that anyone arriving unannounced has been maneuvered here by God and that He has a purpose in them being here. Some, both in Taxila and in Gujranwala, are victims of road accidents along the Grand Trunk Road. They need time to recuperate. For some it proves also a time for personal spiritual reassessment.

Our own guests—we have a number of close friends from our church in the States over the years—can hardly comprehend the relaxed efficiency of Marie's style in running a household of such variable size. She merely sets an extra place at the table if an unknown, a person who had not been there when she went to bed at nine o'clock, emerges from one of the bedrooms for breakfast. Sooner or later someone will explain.

The Bible talks of the value of hospitality for *"thereby some have entertained angels unaware."*

Not all of Marie's guests are angels. Not all of the volunteers who work with us are angels. All however consider Marie to be *in loco materna* and in a strange and fascinating land accept her authority and advice over living arrangements, customs and, particularly for the girls, clothing and behavior. They might be assigned their work by me but in all practical matters they go straight to Marie.

Then there are the unexpected casual drop-ins.

Ron just turns up one day. How he finds us I have no idea but here he is. We are having four o'clock tea. He is in his late thirties I suppose, older than our usual run of foreigners. He is surprised to be welcomed as though he has been expected, given tea and told to bring in his luggage.

Over tea he explains who he is. He isn't a casual drop-in off the Grand Trunk Road. He has come looking for us from Abu Dhabi in the Persian Gulf. He knows our son Colin in England. When he gets a job as a draftsman in Abu Dhabi, Colin gives him our address and says he is sure Mom and Dad will be glad to see him if he is ever our way. I am not sure Colin is aware Abu Dhabi is close to a couple of thousand miles and several countries away. I doubt too that he knows Ron is on drugs. In Abu Dhabi, Ron finds that the job he has been promised is no longer available and hotels are expensive. He has to find a cheaper hotel quickly. He flies to Lahore and finds us.

We assure him that he has not found us but that God has brought him to us. What other kind of work can he do? Well, he has been a professional footballer with Leyton Orient, one of the Football League teams. We now have a new instructor in the drafting shop and, much more important, a footballer.

Few of our volunteers have much to do with the Khokherke boys. Ron is different. He has little to do with the younger volunteers and gravitates naturally to the soccer field after school ends. I encourage the Khokherke boys to use our playing facilities, basketball and soccer. Now they have not only a top-class player but they also have a coach. Ron is similar to Colin, his friends are Pakistani, and he enjoys drinking tea with them in the teashops and visiting their homes. The Khokherke boys love Ron. He is having more influence with them than any other foreigner we have had and it is influence for good.

He stays in one of our guest rooms. I find him there one day on his bed stoned on drugs and sit with him until he comes to. I counsel with him, keep the matter to myself, and accept his assurances (with some reservations) that it will not happen again. Something important—spiritually important—is happening to Ron. He is finding himself loved for himself with an unselfish love. I doubt he has encountered that before but some kind of healing is going on within him and the Khokherke boys are part of the therapy.

When the time comes for Ron to leave, he thinks he will go to the States and look for a job there. He would also like to be our accredited representative to raise funds for us. He can speak with first hand knowledge of what we are doing to help boys in need. I do not follow this offer up, fearing that his drug habit might reappear and our work could be damaged by association. However when he leaves, after the usual round of farewell parties from his students and the Khokherke boys, he leaves a different man than the man who had come.

I wonder what ever happened to Ron?

A Variety of Volunteers

Over the years we notice a distinct change in the young people who are coming to us. We learn much about the current changing standards of the West by observing our latest volunteers and listening to their conversations.

Missionaries inevitably become Rip van Winkles, caught in a time warp. They lose touch with their own countries and its changing mores. Our length of service is five years and furlough still comes around too quickly. We remember London and New York as they were when we were last home and not reckoning on the changes. Each furlough is a crash-learning experience for travelers from antiquity.

Our U.S. Presbyterian Church conducts regular polls on questions it is curious about with its *Presbyterian Panel.* This is a carefully balanced and identified group of people representing various streams in the life of the church. For a while we serve on this panel and observe (or think we observe) where each of these streams fit into the spectrum of opinions.

The most liberal, on the left of center as it were, is the stream of staff opinion in the headquarters of the denomination. One step in is the presbytery and synod staff. A further step towards the center is the general membership of the church. Moving now towards the right are the serving lay elders, then the serving ministers and next the retired ministers. This is, or should have been, disturbing for the church at home. It still struggles with some of the consequences of its leadership not representing the mainline thinking of the denomination but one particular edge of it.

By far the most conservative in outlook, on the far right of the church's opinions, are the serving missionaries. This is to be expected. They are certainly initially conservative in outlook. Furthermore, most of them have been long away from the subtle liberalizing home influences so they are out of date. In the Sialkot Mission, missionaries neither smoke nor drink beer, wine or spirits. They still avoid traveling on Sunday. I doubt whether, as much as they want their Marie back, they would have allowed me in if I had smoked either cigarettes or a pipe.

Their views of sex are biblical. They teach and observe biblical morality and expect it from others. One of our young volunteers proves to be homosexual. We are fighting homosexuality in our boarding dormitories of more than three hundred boys and trying to protect young boys against sexual predators. We don't need his help in that struggle.

Two others, a boy and a girl, think they will spend the night in bed together. That is their last night in Gujranwala. They are perhaps children of their time, but we believe that morality matters and that it will continue to matter.

Drugs are another problem. It isn't a new problem of course. A contemptuous word for Christians generally is *bhangis*—meaning druggies or users of marijuana. This goes way back to the origins of the north Indian Christian community from the outcastes of Hinduism. What is new is the fascination of young westerners with the habit.

Before Pakistan became its own nation, there were probably five particular groups of British in India. There was the military establishment. There was the equivalent and high quality civil establishment involved in government. There were British who had settled and were in business, newspapers and education.

There were the railway people. Many of the British railway workers had taken Indian wives and the Anglo Indian generations had resulted. Then there were the missionaries. Each had its own particular standing. The population knew where each of them fitted and they were treated accordingly.

Then begin to come into the land different kinds of foreigner. Not all are heading for the drug culture of Goa. Some are young and they come to help and not to make money. They are a credit to their home countries. We have the opportunity to observe youngsters like this from two different streams of government sponsored volunteer service.

The Peace Corps, initiated by President Kennedy, taps the energies of America's youth in a variety of forms of overseas service. These are fine young people full of initiative, creativity and energy, willing totally to endure physical hardship and bad living conditions. Many of them suffer continually from dysentery. Their jobs, selected for them by the host country, seem poorly chosen and badly supervised.

We get to know well the Peace Corps volunteers in Sialkot. Keith, who lives on the Wazirabad Road, converts his hobby into a living for others. His assignment is a non-job so with his own money he starts a little industry, Arizona Industries, making tooled leather bags and belts. He seems to live on a continuous diet of brown beans which have to be soaked for many hours before cooking. He is frequently sick. Judy, a nurse, is having her spirit broken in the district hospital as she encounters a culture of bribes for nursing care together with poor nursing practices and even worse sterilizing techniques. Duane tries to persuade peasants there is value in planting rice in straight rows and, at least for one season, succeeds. Harry out at Narowal seems almost abandoned as he tries to work on improving housing.

Each of them finds in Marie a mother spirit. We are living in a house with twenty-one outside doors and a hundred windows. It has once been the home and office of the Deputy Commisioner. There is room enough for these youngsters to come in for a break, to have decent food, safe water and oodles of tender loving care. We actually have, instead of one made of marble chip terrazzo, a cast iron bathtub that I imported from Scotland along with others for the hospital. They love that bathtub! They are welcome from the moment they arrive. Marie nurses them back to health. They can relax, talk, play board games or badminton and then they can grit their teeth and go back to work again. We are awaiting the arrival of a batch of new ones, all young engineers of some kind that I am to orientate into local building methods and techniques. Just then one of our wars (the '65 war) with India erupts and our young Peace Corps friends are gone. They do not return.

The other group is British. The scheme, Volunteer Service Overseas, is on a much smaller scale than the Peace Corps. It is well organized, well supervised by the British Council and the quality of young people is different although certainly not better. These youngsters usually have a religious interest that takes them to church. They are not, like the Peace Corps, assigned to Government offices and agencies in a government-to-government relationship but directly assigned to suitable institutions that can use volunteers. This works much better as far as the volunteers are concerned. The British Council has a direct and positive liaison over welfare and care with the employing institution. Our first VSO's were two young Britons who come to us from Gordon College where they are teaching. The last two are snatched away, protesting, during our war with India in 1971. We are able to remain in Gujranwala while they are evacuated initially to Kabul and then further west.

Farewell to a Stranger

September 1997

Gibbins Brook Farm, Sellindge, Kent U.K.

On the 5th of September, my brother Tony's birthday, Marie dies. Her valiant struggle against cancer is finally over. She has been in the Hospice at Canterbury and dies in her sleep in the early hours of the morning while I hold her hand. Her labored breathing slows and then stops.

Her parents' home was Sweden. Her land of birth was the United States. Her land of labors was Pakistan. And now she is buried in England.

The twelfth century parish church in the English village of Sellindge is full to say farewell to the *Stranger* who for such a short while lives among them. It is an unusual service. Even those with most reason to feel brokenhearted feel not grief but rather surprise as other unknown facets of her life are shared and even a joy, a pride, that they have been privileged to be acquainted with her. They have been asked to come as for a celebration, no dark clothing. They do and it is indeed a celebration they find.

Beneath her name on the order of service is a poem I had written years previously for another "M."

> *Though angels dance with haste and urge me on*
> *Plucking flowers I'll walk the vale along*
> *Gazing at trees and watching waterfalls*
> *When the sun of my day goes down, my dear.*
> *I'll listen for your sweet remembered voice*
> *Calling, calling across the other land,*
> *I'll look for nesting birds, at the turn pause,*
> *Looking back lest your shining hasting form*
> *Slipping noiseless through the perfumed air*
> *Perhaps be unobserved.*
> *And, if come*
> *To journey's end and unaccompanied,*
> *Then, till you come, beside the gate somewhere*
> *I'll find a pleasant place to sit and wait.*
> *One day,*
> *If timeless time breaks down to day,*
> *Dozing in the sun, you'll touch my shoulders*
> *From behind, laughing as you used to laugh,*
> *And then I'll know that you have come*
> *And waiting's done and we are one again.*

As the cortege takes its way from the church it catches the shadows of a yew tree twelve hundred years old in the churchyard.

The final act of farewell to her is a line of people each waiting in silence to throw, not *dust to dust* but a single rose from their gardens onto a gracious lady who has loved roses.

The focal poem of the collection *Footprints in the Dust* is titled *Roses for a Stranger*. It begins

> *Bear the bier slowly,*
> *Throw on a few roses,*
> *Tread the grass gently,*
> *Lonely she goes*
> *At the head of the throng.*
> *Now we walk slowly,*
> *Ahead she goes quickly.*
> *We only are feeling*
> *The cold of the evening,*
> *For her morning's breaking*
> *With glory all round.*
> *We hesitate still,*
> *She's knowing it all.*
> *To affirm is a struggle,*
> *For her there's no question*
> *And she pauses not hasting*
> *For the tears we are crying.*
> *The hours of our questing*
> *She's bequeathed us with gladness*
> *And she's taken with her*
> *The answers she found.*
>
> *She was one of the strange ones*
> *Who live in a larger world*
> *Than the one we know . . .*

One of the richest gifts of life that we can acquire is simply the knowledge that we live in a larger world than that circumscribed by our five senses. There are other senses, ways of awareness that we do have. There are also penetrations into our sensory world that have their origins elsewhere. Together they open the door to a richer way of living and a fulsome sense of purpose along the Way ahead. They enable us to make a difference. There is no need to be satisfied with less!

On Marie's gravestone is inscribed part of a response I wrote to a poem by Gerard Manley Hopkins that he called *A Nun Takes the Veil*

I've no desire to go
Where springs not fail,
To fields where flies
No sharp and sided hail
And a few lilies blow.

I've no desire to be
Where no storms blow,
Where the green swell
Is in the haven dumb
And out of the swing of the sea.

I'll choose instead to be
Where storms rage on,
Where the helpless
In their rage are dumb
And weep in their futility.

Instead my feet shall go
Where stings the hail

And to those lands
Where droughts prevail
And stunted children grow.

And, maybe, a few roses.

I hope there are roses in heaven. Goodbye, *Stranger*.